Not Everyone Will End Up with an Axe in the Forest

Tools for a Better Life in a Chaotic World

Bruno Marion

Copyright Information

Not Everyone Will End Up with an Axe in the Forest
Tools for a Better Life in a Chaotic World

© 2024 Bruno Marion

All rights reserved. No part of this book may be reproduced, distributed, or transmitted in any form or by any means, including photocopying, recording, or other electronic or mechanical methods, without the prior written permission of the publisher, except in the case of brief quotations embodied in critical reviews and certain other noncommercial uses permitted by copyright law. For permission requests, write to the publisher, addressed "Attention: Permissions Coordinator," at the address below.

Publisher: Bruno Marion / KDP

www.brunomarion.com

*To all the young people who have adopted me,
Alexandre, Eliott, Kai, Maria, Parker, Valentin,
and to all the young people who build
a better world.*

Contents

INTRODUCTION Why the world has become more uncertain... and why that's good news! 9
    Why numbers, connection and speed have made our world more uncertain 10
    The human world speeds up 15
    Has the world gone mad? 17
    Why use chaos theories? 18
    Collapse or emergence? 23
    What is emergence? 32
    Chaos is neither good nor bad 36
    So, is it going to go back to the way it was? 37

CHAPTER 1 Long live uncertainty: you've never had so much power! 40
    How to use simplicity in the face of complexity 40
    A pilot shot down in Iraqi desert 42
    Fractal glasses for better vision in a chaotic world 44
    How our own identity became fractal... 52
    From the clash of civilizations to the clash for a civilization 54
    How can you organize your life in a fractal way? 58
    Towards fractal energy networks? 59
    Fractal companies and organizations? 60

CHAPTER 2 How to build, clarify and realize your dreams with chaos theories 62

How to choose what happens in your life, even if you can no longer predict precisely 62
What is chaos?.. 63
What is a strange attractor and how can you use it? 64
Your dream... or someone else's 65
How do you create your strange attractor? 66
2ᵉ step: take a picture of the present and ensure the transition to the future 70
How do you manage your dreams as a family or team? 77
How does it work? 77

CHAPTER 3 How to make big changes with small changes in your life 80

The butterfly effect: the secret of big results from small actions 80
Understanding self-amplification 83
You've never had so much power! 86
How to create emergences, radical transformations in your life 88
Visualize your vision, your dreams, your strange attractor 89
How to define your daily "ritual of success" 90
Why talk about exponential routines? 91
My ritual of success 91
E-mails... 96
And when I don't even have five minutes: the express ritual 97
Your mindset pack 98
How to reprogram your brain to overcome your limiting beliefs 99
Create your new Personnal Operating System 104
A special case: information processing 113
How others can help you realize your dreams 119
The 3-2-1: the way to avoid being stuck in the past 122
Weekly Review 126
Playing together: group routines 128
How to surround yourself with reliable people 133
My tips for getting started 135

Conclusion 137

Appendix Why and how to prepare for crises? 139

Equipment and survival 140
Relational and emotional level 141

Meaning level 143
Thanks **147**
Bibliography **148**
Complexity, Uncertainty, and Chaos Theory.. 148
Sociology and Understanding the Modern World 150
Integral Theory 155

YOUR EXCLUSIVE BONUSES

Thank you for buying the book !

To thank you in my own way, visit brunomarion.com//bonus-book/ to receive your bonuses:

- practical tools for applying the book to your own life

- the list of the best resources I recommend you follow

- answers to readers' questions (you can ask me your own), regularly updated to go even further than the book's content.

And I have a few more surprises in store for you...

Visit brunomarion.com/bonus-book/ to receive all the book's bonuses (and much more!).

INTRODUCTION

Why the world has become more uncertain... and why that's good news!

"The problem with our times is that the future isn't what it used to be."
Paul Valéry

The world is in crisis... At least, that's what we hear every day on TV, on the radio, in the newspapers, on social networks or from friends!

But while everyone's talking about possible crises and probable collapse, few are talking about possible opportunities and probable emergence. The new world and how to get there. That's what this book is all about.

One day, at the end of an interview, the journalist from a major national radio station asked me: "If there was only one thing to do to prevent the world from collapsing, what would it be?" After a few seconds of thought (and doubt about my ability to answer such a question...), I answer her what then seems obvious to me: "Say hello to your neighbor every day. Really, every day." Like her, aren't you convinced that a small action can change the world? I don't blame you, I've had my doubts too. The aim of this book is to show you that, paradoxically, in this world where everything has become more uncertain and chaotic, you've never had so much power over your own life.

This book aims to show you why and how we're going through a genuine metamorphosis of a scale and speed unprecedented in human history... and that this can be good news. It shares a new, accessible, immediately applicable model that will enable you to navigate uncertainty, be more resilient and even take advantage of crises!

We will look at why and how our world has become more uncertain, what practical tools you need to surf the tsunami of change, and above all, why you've never had so much power to make your dreams come true. This book won't just help you understand the future, it will give you the tools you need to build the future you want for yourself, for our organizations, for the world we leave to our children... and so that we don't all end up with an axe at the bottom of the forest.

Why numbers, connection and speed have made our world more uncertain

When I meet someone who asks me what I do for a living (we'll see in the 3rd chapter of this book that it's important to know how to answer this type of question to help others... to help you), I usually reply: "My mission is to convince people who aren't yet convinced that we (humans) are living through a transition unprecedented in human history. And that this transition can be good news if we understand it." My mission is also to find and share the tools to surf the tsunami of changes we are going through and will continue to go through and leave a better world to our children."

I readily admit that it's a bit ambitious... even pretentious! And most of the time, my interlocutors are quick to remind me that not only is it ambitious, it's also pointless! So, one of the objections I hear most often is: "You think this is an exceptional time, that we're living through an incredible transition, because it's YOUR time. 100 years ago, or 1,000 years ago, or 10,000 years ago, humans must also have thought they were living in incredible times!" Objections that take different forms, but that can be summed up as: that's the way it was before! If someone says that to you, I invite you to tell him or her that he or she is right! Because, of course, our ancestors have lived through transitions, crises, wars, chosen or forced migrations and (already!)

pandemics. And of course, nature and the living world have always presented chaotic aspects. The difference with our transition can be summed up in three words: numbers, connection and speed.

NUMBERS

How many people were on Earth 150 years ago? About a billion. How many are we today? Over eight billion. Over the last few years, in just a few generations, the population has grown at an incredible rate. In fact, we're talking about a veritable explosion! If our ancestors lived in a relatively empty world, we live in a very, very full one! A world that's full and, as we shall see, highly connected.

The global population explosion

THE CONNECTION

On August 4, 1938, an expedition from the American Museum of Natural History on an exploratory mission in search of new bird species in New Guinea was to change human history. Entering the Great Balim River Valley, then thought to be uninhabited, they discovered a population of over 50,000 people! Richard Archbold's expedition was to achieve what may well have been the last *first encounter*. For one of the last times in the history of mankind, it was to bring together men and women who were unaware of the existence of other men and women elsewhere on Earth! This is unlikely to happen again today...

Humans are increasingly rubbing shoulders and meeting each other. And our frustration at not being able to do so was brutally exposed during what we'll call *the confinement period*. Humans are also communicating more and more:

- more than half of the human population has access to the Internet, increasingly via a smartphone;
- there are more cell phones on Earth than human beings since 2014! More people on Earth have a cell phone than have a bank account, or access to drinking water or a toilet.

I've noticed that not only are we communicating more and more, but we're also more and more aware of belonging to a human community.

One evening in August 1997, I was driving home from dinner with a friend who was living on a barge on the Seine near the Bir-Hakeim bridge in Paris. On the quays of the right bank, we reached the Alma tunnel: impossible to use, as it was closed. We then watch the chase between a policeman trying to tackle, rugby-style, what appears to be a journalist, or at least someone with many cameras. As we reach the other side of the tunnel, we see dozens of police, fire and ambulance vehicles with their lights on. Gas leak? A terrorist attack? Actually, a car accident in a Paris tunnel. For those of you who haven't watched television in over twenty years, Princess Diana had just died.

Some time later, an estimated 2.5 billion people in over 190 countries watched Lady Di's funeral on television in 44 languages. This represented 40% of humanity at the time. Even if other estimates are much lower, counting only 500 million viewers, this would still be one of the most watched events on television! So, an unprecedented number of people in human history gathered around the disappearance of a woman they had never met, as if she were one of their neighbors or a member of their family...

> **Six degrees of separation**
>
> You may have heard the term "six degrees of separation". The idea is that every person in the world is connected to every other person by fewer than six social connections. Researchers tested this in the 1960s and found it to be pretty much true.
>
> In the age of social media, one would assume that since we all know so many more people from so many different parts of the world, there would be fewer connections between any two random people. Who better to analyze this than Facebook? After analyzing 721 million people and their connections, Facebook discovered that in 2016, on average, two people in the world are separated by 3.57 people. So we can now speak of "three point fifty-seven degrees of separation"...
>
> (https://research.facebook.com/blog/2016/02/three-and-a-half-degrees-of-separation/)

On December 26, 2004, I was in India on the road between Chennai and Pondicherry when a journalist from a major all-news french radio station called me from Paris on my French cell phone, unaware that I was in India, to ask my opinion of the *situation*. That's how I learned that I was in the part of India most affected by the tsunami, which claimed 225,000 lives and left millions homeless in Asia.

Within hours, thousands of videos had already been posted on the Internet, triggering an outpouring of emotion and solidarity never before seen in human history. Never before had so many people come to the aid of people they had never met.

Could this unprecedented outpouring of generosity be a sign that humanity has begun to realize its own dimension on a planetary scale? Is it a sign of what we call an "emergence", which I'm going to tell you about in a few lines?

In short, remember that there have never been so many of us on Earth, and we've never been so connected to each other! As David Ruelle, one of the first scientists to talk about chaos theories, writes: "The more oscillators [that's what he calls the different elements of a system] and the more interconnections between them, the more we should be ready to see chaos."

SCALE AND SPEED

Why is the transition we're going through unlike any previously experienced by Humanity? The answer is scale and speed. No other transition affecting humanity has affected so many people on Earth in such a short space of time.

A more connected world that is also moving faster and faster:

- the evolution of the lithosphere (the mineral) is counted in billions of years;
- the evolution of the biosphere (living organisms) is measured in millions of years;
- the evolution of the noosphere (information) is counted in nanoseconds!

At the very level of human history, if it took thousands of years for man to move from the hunting-gathering era to the farming-breeding era, and hundreds of years to move into the industrial-commercial era, it's only a few decades that have brought us to the era we'll call the creative-communication, information or knowledge era.

And, very importantly, the major transitions from hunting and gathering to agriculture and livestock, and from agriculture and livestock to industry and trade, did not affect everyone at the same time. These transitions were spread out over time and geographically.

Most of today's technological, social and economic revolutions are taking place within a single generation. Human beings and cultures no longer have the time to adapt smoothly. For example, our grandparents were born, worked and died near the same geographical location, whereas the probability of being born, working and dying in the same place is now almost nil for most of us! Similarly, the 1,000 words of common language that our parents learned were, with a few exceptions, the same 1,000 words they used at the end of their lives. The 1,000 words you most commonly use are already a far cry from those you learned when you were younger. Not so long ago, you weren't downloading, chatting, tweeting, podcasting, posting, zooming or e-mailing much either...

> **We no longer speak the same language!**
>
> Even our language is changing faster and faster. From one generation to the next, we no longer understand each other! Since Richelieu, the Académie française has published a dictionary as a reference approximately every twenty years. In previous centuries, the difference between two publications was around 4,000 to 5,000 words, a figure that has remained more or less constant; between the previous one and the next, it will be around 30,000. At this rate, we can guess that our successors could soon find themselves as separated from our language as we are from the old French spoken centuries ago..

Thirty years ago, I used the first cell phone. It was the size of a small suitcase...

The transition we've been experiencing for the past few decades is affecting almost everyone at the same time! Today's technological, social and economic revolutions are taking place over two or even just one generation. No technological revolution has affected so many human beings in such a short space of time!

And that changes everything...

The human world speeds up

In 2020, I return to France from Thailand on March 16... the day before the lockdown. Just enough time to reach my resilient home and my little family in the South of France. Many of the friends, clients and journalists I've met in the past then remember that I've been working on uncertainty and crisis management for over twenty years. And they all ask me for advice. Many of the people I talk to also ask, "Don't you think this is all just *a little flu?*" And many make comparisons with the Spanish flu, or even older pandemics that were even more deadly. Obviously, I couldn't comment on the seriousness of the new disease. Unlike many people at the time, I hadn't certified myself as an epidemiologist after reading three Facebook articles and watching two YouTube videos... However, it was already clear to me that the consequences would go beyond those of a simple flu.

By the end of March, a few hundred thousand deaths had been attributed to Covid (then known as coronavirus), perhaps more in reality. By the end of April, just a few weeks later, more than half the human population was under some form of confinement. More than 4 billion people saw their daily, professional and family lives radically changed in just a few weeks! Many people still say to me: "It's the media's fault", "It's social networks' fault", "It's the evolution of our relationship with death's fault", and so on. This may be true... but it's also missing out on an incredible phenomenon: in the space of a few weeks, the daily lives of several billion human beings have been significantly impacted. Even during the two world wars a large proportion of human beings weren't even aware that these wars were taking place on the other side of the planet. Similarly, with the Spanish flu, it took decades to realize the impact and death of 50 to 100 million people. At the time, people weren't aware of the catastrophe, but unlike Covid, the Spanish flu didn't impact half the world's population in a matter of weeks. The number of cases was not tracked daily on Twitter or Facebook...

The scale and speed of Covid's impact on the human population is a perfect example of the butterfly effect or self-amplification described in chaos theories, and which we will learn to use to our advantage in the third chapter of this book.

So yes, certain aspects of human life are speeding up. If an Italian peasant from 1300 could find himself in Tuscany in the 1870s, thanks to a time machine, he wouldn't notice many differences... Conversely, if you knew China thirty years ago and went back there today, I can assure you that you wouldn't recognize anything.

Added to all this acceleration is the incredible friction between things that evolve very quickly and things that cannot evolve very quickly (for the time being?):

- it still takes about nine months to make a child;
- it still takes between fifteen and twenty-five years to make an adult;
- it still takes a season to grow certain fruits and vegetables;
- it takes several years for a fruit tree to start producing fruit;
- Even if we were to immediately and completely halt our CO_2 emissions, it would take thousands of years to dissipate the CO_2 produced over the last three hundred years.

So, I think it's safe to say that we're going through a transition, or rather several transitions, on a scale and at a speed never before seen in human history. Because there have never been so many of us on Earth, because we have never been so interconnected, and because a number of phenomena are accelerating, we are experiencing an unprecedented transition.

Has the world gone mad?

Let's say it's gone out of "equilibrium". The increase in the number of people on Earth, the increase in the number of connections and speed, leads to what scientists call a "non-linear", turbulent, or even chaotic state. And we're going to see that this can be good news!

Humanity is faced with increasingly extreme situations, particularly in the social, economic and, even more dramatically for the long term, ecological spheres. These are what we more commonly call "crises". Crises that are self-amplifying, creating a systemic crisis in which one leads to another, which in turn exacerbates the first, and so on in a vicious circle.

For example, each of these three problems - nuclear war (the almost forgotten threat that is reappearing on Europe's doorstep or in the Taiwan Strait...); ecological collapse (climate disruption, collapse of biodiversity, depletion of natural resources, new pandemics, etc.) and technological risks (the emergence of increasingly totalitarian states through control of our data, the uncontrolled explosion of Terminator-style artificial intelligence, the downgrading of the human being, etc.) is enough to threaten the future of human civilization. But taken together, they represent an unprecedented existential crisis, not least because they are likely to reinforce and combine with each other. In other words, these problems are not independent of each other, but rather interconnected. For example, a nuclear war could trigger a major ecological crisis, leading to considerable technological disruption. Similarly, technological disruption could cause ecological collapse, which in turn could lead to nuclear war.

Since the end of the Second World War, our parents and grandparents, whatever their country of origin, culture or religion, all shared one belief: they believed in progress. They were almost all convinced that their children - that's us!- would live in a world better than theirs. We're the first generation of human beings in several generations to believe (ask around...) that we're going to leave future generations - our children - a planet in worse shape than ours, and that our own actions will not ensure their survival with any certainty.

Survivalism courses are packed. Billionaires are buying huge estates in New Zealand, supposedly the country the most remote from today's follies and risks. I wouldn't be surprised if the Cold War fallout shelters we used to talk about when I was young were back in vogue... Everybody take cover and save yourselves! We'll all end up with an axe deep in the forest, eating wild herbs and lighting ourselves with candles (if there are any left...).

In short: things are bad... but they can be better!

Indeed, according to chaos theories, two scenarios are possible: either everything collapses, or a new civilization emerges! Humanity has reached a fork in the road. We are in a period of complete redefinition of norms and values in terms of work, the economy and social life. Or put more simply: how do we want to live together?

As I said earlier, my mission is to convince those who are not yet convinced that we are living through a transition unprecedented in human history. So, I hope you can now help me in this mission by reminding you: it's the scale and speed of this transition that changes everything. My mission is also to find and share the tools to surf the tsunami of changes we are going through in order to leave a better world to our children. And that's what this book is all about.

> **VUCA or FANI?**
>
> More and more people are talking about the "VUCA" (*Volatility, Uncertainty, Complexity* and *Ambiguity*) world. Personally, I think that the VUCA world is already outdated, and that we should instead speak of the FANI world, which stands for Fragile, Anxiogenic, Non-linear and Incomprehensible...

Why use chaos theories?

Among the glasses and paradigms we use to see and understand the world, three have held an essential place over the centuries: spirituality or religions, philosophy and science. While religion was predominant for centuries, science has taken its revenge over the last two hundred years. So much so, in fact, that it has often eliminated the others... So if science has taken such an important place in our way of seeing and understanding the world, the least we can do is check that our scientific "glasses" are up to date!

Well, our current scientific glasses are perfectly suited to a stable world, close to equilibrium or not too far from it. They're also perfectly suited to a binary world, true/false, good/evil, and so on. But the world is no longer stable. It has moved out of equilibrium, and in many areas has become turbulent and chaotic. It is therefore necessary to abandon a linear and binary vision, and instead develop a vision adapted to this new world. To do this, I'd like to start by showing you how our vision of the world is linked, among other things, to the scientific paradigm of each era. Let's take a look at the main scientific revolutions.

It's hard to pinpoint a starting date, so I suggest the invention of the wheel as the beginning of our technical and scientific adventure. This can be dated back some 5,000 years. As we can see with the wheel, great scientific revolutions sometimes take a long time to be understood and to spread, since it took almost 5,000 years to put one under our suitcases!

First revolution: how long does it take to fill your bathtub?

The first major scientific revolution was undoubtedly initiated by Newton, with his so-called "classical mechanics". With Newton, we discovered that nature is comprehensible. It is also predictable. One of the essential points of classical mechanics is that if we know the state of a system (positions and velocities of its various points) at the initial instant, we can calculate how this state varies over time, and thus determine the state of this system at any other instant. This is also why we speak of a deterministic vision: if you know the initial conditions, you'll know the system's evolution with certainty. The Cosmos is an immense machine whose every aspect, transformation and evolution we can understand and predict in absolute time and space.

The principles of classical, Newtonian mechanics are still the main paradigm, the main glasses, that we use to understand the world. And let's face it, there's nothing like classical mechanics to tell us how long it takes to fill a bathtub, or when two trains are going to pass each other. Most of us have mastered the essential principles. We humans have long been under the impression that if we can simply understand the immutable laws of how things happen, we'll be perfectly capable of predicting, planning and managing the future. So we've made it our duty to find out how things happen, by discovering the laws and patterns that govern our world. Our tacit contract with the universe has been that if we work hard enough and think clearly enough, the universe will deliver its secrets, because the universe is knowable, and therefore at least somewhat flexible to our will. Classical mechanics is thus perfectly suited to analyzing, understanding and acting on phenomena at or close to equilibrium. It will help us, for example, to understand the different forces at play when we study a table placed on the floor (in equilibrium). It will also help us understand an oscillating system close to equilibrium, such as a pendulum.

In many everyday expressions, we can see how our thinking, our vision of the world, is influenced by classical mechanics: "I've found a good balance", "He's unbalanced", "It's always been like this, it's not going to change now", "It's all cyclical, it'll come back", "Watch out for the pendulum swinging back", "The wheel is turning", etc.

Second revolution: everything is relative!

Just over a hundred years ago, two revolutions in scientific thinking took place within a few years of each other: relativity and quantum mechanics.

The second major scientific revolution after Newton: Einstein's relativity. We learned some astonishing things. Nothing can go faster than the speed of light. The closer we get to the speed of light, the more time slows down. The sun bends the rays of light. Nothing can come out of a black hole. And so on... Above all, space and time are no longer absolute, as Newton stated. They are interrelated and can differ according to the observer. Einstein became more famous than a rock star. Even those who didn't understand his theories of special and general relativity understood that the world would never be the same again. The glasses have changed irrevocably, and the consequences of these changes will sometimes extend far beyond the realms of science. And here too, ordinary people are reappropriating what they have understood, or think they have understood, from the theories of relativity, and using it in language in the same way as when we say, "Everything is relative."

Third revolution: a quantum leap

Around the same time (what a time!), a third revolution in scientific thought took place, with Heisenberg, Planck, Bohr, de Broglie, Born, Schrödinger and others initiating what would come to be known as quantum mechanics. More and more astonishing things continued to emerge. For example, we learn that light can be a wave or a particle. Or that, contrary to classical deterministic mechanics, we can't know both the speed and position of something. Or that the probability of my going through a wall without damage to myself or the wall is not zero (don't try this at home, the probability isn't very high either...). This is the entry of probability into the previously deterministic world. It's impossible to predict exactly when and how certain phenomena will occur. It is only possible to know their probability.

Relativity was already a revolution in thinking, but at least it had the courtesy to preserve the rule of cause and effect. This is no longer the case with quantum mechanics, which calls it partly into question. Chance is beginning to make its grand entrance. Another wall of classical thinking collapses. And once again, this is reflected in expressions used in everyday language, for example: "It's a real quantum leap."

Fourth revolution: chaos theories

The latest and most recent major scientific revolution: the theories of chaos, turbulent systems and non-linear systems.

How old is chaos theory? It's hard to say. Indeed, while it's easy to date Mandelbrot's creation of the word "fractal", for example, many pieces of the puzzle had been observed long before by Poincaré, of course, but also Maxwell and even Einstein. So, when the new discoveries in chaos theory first appeared, few people knew how to make the connection. Mathematicians made a discovery in mathematics, while physicists made a discovery in physics, while meteorologists made a discovery in meteorology, and so on. In the same way, it's difficult to attribute the invention of chaos theories to a single person, as with classical mechanics (Newton) or relativity (Einstein), or to a limited number of people, as with quantum mechanics. With chaos theories, there is no longer any unity of person, place, time or even scientific field. People like Poincaré, Lorentz, Feigenbaum, Yorke, Ruelle,

Mandelbrot, Prigogine, etc. are involved in fields as different and sometimes as far apart as mathematics, physics, meteorology, finance, hydraulics, biology and so on. So we had to wait for the emergence of true integrators of thought, specialists in systemics and epistemology such as Ilya Prigogine and Isabelle Stengens, Edgar Morin and Erwin Lazslo, before we really saw the coherence of the whole and its applications to the evolution of our vision of the world. It could also be said that, while previous scientific revolutions have been fairly linear and binary (pre-Newton and post-Newton, pre-Einstein and post-Einstein), chaos theory has appeared more like a "fractal" puzzle that has been unfolding over the last forty years or so, and will surely continue to unfold in other fields. Chaos theory, which we'll finally and somewhat arbitrarily date to the late 1970s, is one of the first developments in science to affect as many different fields as finance, weather forecasting, or even more recent sciences such as neuroscience. Even today, chaos theory remains the least developed theoretically, empirically studied and practically applied. In this sense, it represents the most promising field for new ideas, techniques and applications. Chaos theory presents a new understanding of reality and our responsiveness to it. Its applications continue to extend to a wide range of human activities, far beyond its origins in mathematics and physics.

Why are chaos theories important to you?

Classical mechanics can be said to be on a human scale. It enables us to analyze systems and phenomena that are not too far from the human scale, neither too small nor too large. Classical, linear mechanics is thus perfectly suited to analyzing phenomena at our own scale, to understanding and acting in a world at, or close to, equilibrium. Also, because, among other reasons, we were relatively few on Earth and communicated relatively little compared to today, the glasses of classical, Newtonian mechanics were perfectly suited. We'll see that, while Newtonian mechanics remains ideal for understanding systems and phenomena in equilibrium or oscillating close to equilibrium, it is no longer at all suited to a world that has become chaotic and turbulent.

On the other hand, relativity and quantum mechanics don't really deal with phenomena on a human scale. In fact, it seems to me that most of us are a long way from mastering all these concepts. Relativity deals mainly with the very, very large and the very, very fast. So, unless you travel at the speed of light, or live close to a black hole - which most of us don't - Einstein's new insights, essential though they are from a philosophical and spiritual point of view, won't necessarily change your understanding of everyday life. It should be noted, however, that the indirect consequences are nonetheless very real, with energy or nuclear weapons for example. We can simplify matters by saying that the theory of relativity doesn't really apply to the human scale, but rather to the infinitely large or the very fast.

Quantum mechanics, on the other hand, deals with the very, very small. And the insights it brings, essential though they may be from a philosophical and spiritual point of view, are not going to change your understanding of everyday life either. And, as with relativity, there are obviously very few of us who have mastered all its concepts. The consequences for our daily lives are still not dramatic although the indirect consequences are also starting to be important, with the transistor, the laser, etc. To simplify, we can say that quantum mechanical theories don't apply directly to the human scale, but rather to the infinitely small.

Unlike relativity and quantum mechanics, chaos theories deal with everything from the infinitely small to the infinitely large... and that includes the human dimension. So they can help us gain new insights into our chaotic world.

Collapse or emergence?

In one of his short stories, visionary science-fiction writer Isaac Asimov tells us the story of a people who, generation after generation, civilization after civilization, ask a giant computer: "Will we ever be able to beat the second principle of thermodynamics?" And for generations and generations, centuries and centuries, the computer systematically answers the same thing: "The data are not sufficient to answer this question." Billions of years pass, stars and galaxies die, but the computer, directly connected to the energy of space-time, continues to calculate. In the end, the universe is dead, but the computer finally arrives at its answer. It now knows how to beat the second principle... and that's when a new universe is born.

Entropy (loosely translated as the measure of disorder) reigns, and nothing escapes the implacable grip of the second law of thermodynamics. That's what we learned at school: with every passing moment, our world, our solar system, indeed our entire galaxy, moves ever closer to its inevitable demise at the end of time. Warm water doesn't naturally separate into hot water on one side and cold water on the other. A broken egg will not reconstitute itself. The disorder can only increase. All previous civilizations have collapsed (the Mayas, Easter Island, the Roman Empire, etc.). Everything will return to dust.

Civilizations, in particular, are very fragile constructions. They rest on a set of beliefs shared by their people. Their belief in the rightness of their values, their belief in the strength of their system of law and order, and perhaps above all, their belief in their future - what we'll call in the rest of this book a "dream" or "strange attractor". All it takes for this belief to evaporate is for the edifice to rapidly collapse, as history is littered with examples.

But chaos theories teach us that this inevitable return to disorder, the predicted collapse, is only part of the story! They do not call into question the second principle of thermodynamics. They do not deny that everything will return to dust, but they also show us an incredible emergence of complexity since the beginning of the universe. Evolutionary biologists generally tend to deny any kind of direction or intention to evolution, seeing it all as a random series of events and blind natural selection. But this point of view is merely a vestige of the reductionist scientific materialism of the XIXe century. It overlooks more current scientific concepts, starting with Ilya Prigogine's Nobel Prize-winning discoveries that even non-living material systems have an inherent tendency towards self-organization. As we'll see later, when physical systems are pushed "far from equilibrium", they escape disorder by leaping into a higher state of organized order. If non-living matter intrinsically possesses this self-organizing drive, living systems certainly do. From the dawn of time, where there seemed to be nothing but a vacuum, matter appeared, then life, then consciousness. The universe has never stopped growing in complexity! It has never stopped evolving. Man and humanity have done the same. So, while many civilizations have collapsed, the "human civilization", the *Homo Sapiens* civilization, is still thriving (at least if you're reading this book) and, as we shall see, has only grown in complexity.

From atoms to molecules, from single-cell organisms to multi-cell organisms, from the reptilian brain to the mammalian brain to the human neocortex, the universe has never ceased to demonstrate inexhaustible creativity. It has never ceased to integrate what exists, to grow in complexity and evolve, through the mineral and the living, towards greater consciousness, towards more beauty, truth and goodness. Evolution, self-organization, integration and emergence are "the other part of the story". And we are living in a unique moment when humanity, itself the product of billions of years of evolution, suddenly becomes aware of this evolutionary process. Chaos theories provide us with essential elements for understanding how we can encourage this evolution towards greater complexity (volunteers for the return to death and dust?) They show us how a system can evolve either towards greater entropy or towards greater complexity. They also allow us, with a radically new way of seeing the world, to participate in this evolution.

This is the first time in human history that man has realized that he is both spectator and actor in the evolution of the universe!

Let's take a look at the three states a system can have, using a classic example used in chaos theory to understand the evolution of turbulent or chaotic systems: water flowing from the tap. Try it out at home (it's even easier to observe with a river... but it's more complicated to do in an apartment!).

THE BALANCE

If you open a faucet very gently, you'll probably be able to get a steady, seemingly immobile flow of water. This is known as the "stationary", "linear" or "laminar" state. If, with great care, you continue to slowly open the tap, you may be able to observe a slight, regular pulsation of the water column. This is the "oscillating" or "periodic" state. If you continue to open the tap, the pulsation will become irregular, and if you open the tap even wider, the flow will become turbulent. Increase the flow. At a certain point, the trickle will turn into a totally chaotic torrent. This is the turbulent or chaotic state. It's chaos! But don't stop there! If you increase the flow even further, a surprising phenomenon can occur. Vortices may appear. Order emerges from chaos. Order emerges from disorder!

We can illustrate these phenomena in simplified terms with the diagrams below.

A system can be stable, in equilibrium (symbolized here by a straight line): it doesn't move, it doesn't evolve.

Balance - equilibrium

Then, at a certain point, the system may start to oscillate, like the tap water described above, or like a pendulum. This is the part symbolized by a sinusoid in the diagrams below. In this part, the system is still under some form of control. There are negative feedback effects. It's like a thermostat. If the heat rises above a certain temperature, the heating is turned off. Similarly, if the temperature drops too low, the heating is turned back on.

Oscillation close to equilibrium

The physical sciences, and our way of seeing the world in general, tend to focus on systems in equilibrium or close to equilibrium. These systems behave in a predictable, linear fashion, which enables the sciences to deal with them. They always return to their predictable initial state. For example, if you touch the pendulum of a clock, it will resume its initial oscillation after a certain amount of time. Once we understand how a system in equilibrium or oscillating close to equilibrium works, we can predict and control it.

But let's see what happens when we move away from equilibrium...

THE TIPPING POINT

At the start of what we'll call "the Covid crisis" in 2020, the questions I was asked most were:

- **Will it return to the way it was?**
- **Will it be better afterwards?**

Let's see how chaos theories can help us answer this kind of question.

Above a certain threshold, known as the "*tipping point*", the system can move out of equilibrium. Oscillations then become increasingly amplified. And chaos theories teach us that once beyond this point, the system can never return to its previous equilibrium. There are what we call "positive feedback effects". The phenomenon is self-amplifying. The higher the temperature, the more you turn up the heat. There are many examples of positive feedback in physical, biological and social systems. For example, positive feedback is at the origin of our birth: the pressure of the baby's head stimulates uterine contractions. The contractions push the head further, further increasing the contractions. The positive feedback thus contributes to the expulsion of the baby from the uterus. And here we are, a few years later, writing or reading books about the future of the world!

> **The tipping point in the ethnic breakdown of neighborhoods**
>
> Malcolm Gladwell has written the bestseller *The Tipping Point*. In it, he describes, with an accumulation of historical examples and detailed explanations, how a great many social processes (fashions, changes in attitudes, crime rates, revolutions, epidemics) emerge in the form of a snowball effect. The notion of the tipping point, he writes, is based on this possible suddenness of change, undoubtedly the most difficult idea to accept. The term 'tipping point' was first used in the 1970s to describe the white suburban rush in the northeastern United States. When the number of African-Americans in a neighborhood reached a certain point - say, 20% - most whites left immediately. The community, sociologists observed, tipped over. The tipping point is a threshold, a boiling point, the moment when a critical mass is reached."
>
> This can also be seen on the positive side: in effect, it means that the switch to much greener policies and practices does not require the entire population to be convinced of its necessity, but only 10 to 15%, a proportion that corresponds to a *tipping point* towards the generalization of a new paradigm...

Let's also look at the creation of a social network such as Facebook, Instagram or TikTok. If few people use it, few people will want to join. On the other hand, the more your friends use it, the more tempted you are to join. The more people use it, the more people want to use it, and the more people use it, and so on... Positive feedback is therefore an accentuation, an amplification, an acceleration of a process by itself upon itself: population growth, thermonuclear reaction, compound interests, economic depression, crowd panic, and so on. In everyday language, we sometimes also speak of a vicious or virtuous circle, depending on whether we like the acceleration of effects or not...

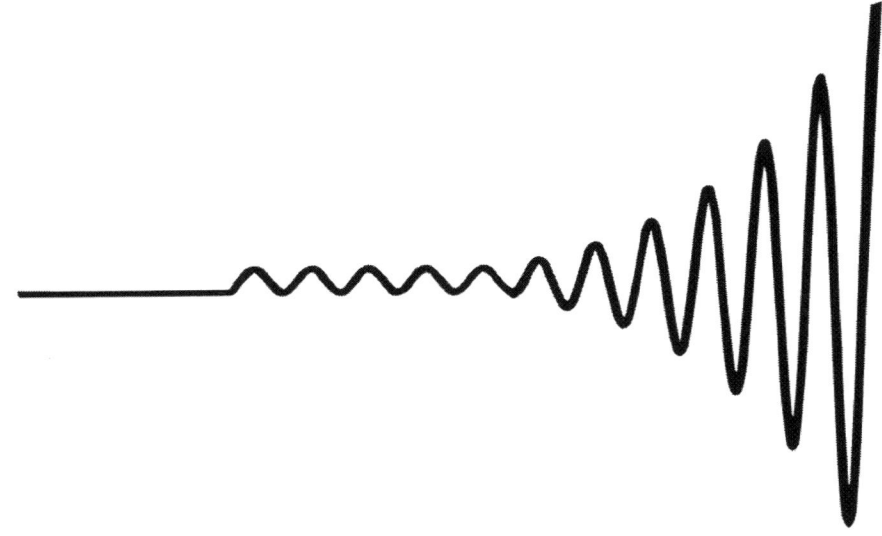

Tipping point and auto-amplification

The "Oh shit" of climate

Hans Joachim Schellnhuber, founder of the Potsdam Institute for Climate Impact Research, was one of the first scientists to analyze the phenomenon of climate tipping points. Some fifteen years ago, the pieces of the puzzle fell into place in his mind: "It was like saying to myself: Oh shit! I realized that the planetary machinery - the monsoons, the ocean circulation, the jet stream, the large ecosystems - is full of non-linear systems. That's why there are so many points of no return. It's like uncorking a bottle, and we're uncorking them one after the other."

Antarctic ice shelves, for example, the extension of glaciers onto the ocean, are being weakened by global warming. If they give way, huge glaciers could be precipitated into the water, raising sea levels by several meters. In the Arctic, permafrost - permanently frozen ground - is thawing. This could eventually release into the atmosphere billions of tons of CO_2, or even worse, methane, which is currently stored there. Another carbon sink threatened by global warming is the rainforest. The Brazilian Amazon recently became a net emitter of CO_2.

Some want to believe that this concept of rupture can be translated in a more positive way in the fight against the climate crisis. This is what researchers call a "sociological tipping point", when a social and/or economic movement becomes irreversible and enough people have become aware of what's at stake and want to take positive action.

THE COLLAPSE

And finally, after equilibrium, oscillation and leaving equilibrium, what happens? Then, after the so-called "decision point", there are two possibilities: the first possibility is that the system collapses. The second principle of thermodynamics applies: everything will return to dust.

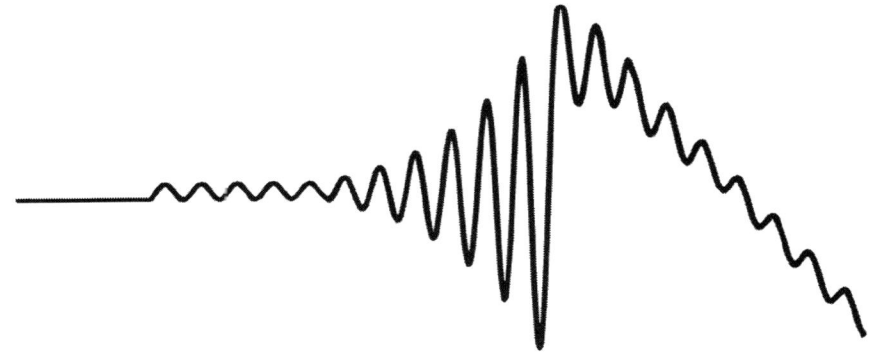

The collapse

The collapse of Rome

The first city in the world to reach a population of one million seems to be the city of Rome. This gives an idea of the complexity the Romans had achieved by then. They were able to feed, transport and organize the lives of a million inhabitants. When Rome collapsed in around 450 AD, the population, according to some estimates, fell from one million to 30,000 in less than thirty years. When it collapses, it does collapse! Note that, at the time, this collapse hardly affected the Indians or the Chinese. This collapse, despite the size of the Roman Empire, remained fairly localized. And another important point is that, if Rome wasn't built in a day, it wasn't defeated in a day either - it took thirty years. Given the number of human beings on Earth today, and their connections, we can imagine that a similar collapse today would not be so localized, but would affect the whole of humanity... and would not take thirty years!

THE EMERGENCE

But there's another possibility, according to chaos theories. Emergence may occur, and the system may find a new equilibrium at a higher level of complexity. Examples are the evolution of living organisms, which we'll describe in the next paragraph, and of the universe in general: from atoms to molecules, from single-cell organisms to multi-cell organisms, from the reptilian brain to the mammalian brain, right up to the human neocortex: the system integrates what already exists and self-organizes to grow in complexity:

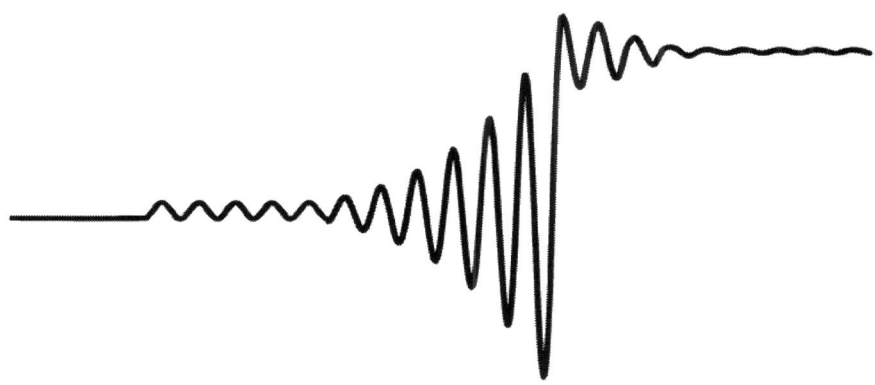

The emergence

Personal collapse

This pattern of collapse or emergence can easily be applied to our personal lives. I remember with great emotion a participant in one of my seminars who, when I was presenting this evolution of emergence or collapse, said to the other participants: "I've been through something similar and I'd like to share it with you". He then told us how he had accompanied his very young son, who was suffering from an incurable disease, until the latter's death. He told us how his life seemed to be in balance, only to be turned upside down by the discovery of his son's illness, and how he, his wife and the rest of the family went through hopes and disappointments, ups and downs of ever-increasing extremes. And finally, he told us how this experience almost drove him into depression and collapse, but how, in the end, he feels today how this experience has helped him evolve in life and how today, along with the sadness that is always present, he also feels a great deal of gratitude for everything that has happened to him and enabled him to evolve.

Touched at the same time by the horror of his story and the relevance of his example to my subject, I've rarely found it so difficult to get on with the rest of my seminar...

Since then, many other people have told me that they have had a similar experience. For example, Donald Meichenbaum, a trauma researcher with fifty years' experience, has stated that of all people who experience trauma, he estimates that 30% suffer from post-traumatic shock, and that 70% experience some form of growth, of personal evolution following the traumatic event.

What is emergence?

The increase in complexity with each emergence is an important point, so what is complexity? And what is emergence?

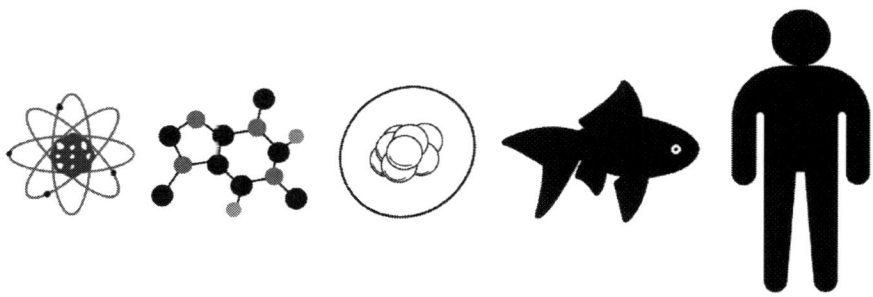

Emergences in the living world

Emergence comes from the study of complex adaptive systems (ant colonies, neural networks, the immune system, the Internet, the global economy). It describes systems whose complex behavior is more than the sum of its simple parts. Think of board games like chess - a few dozen rules governing just 64 squares somehow produce possibilities we're still discovering after two centuries of study. Or think of a seed: it contains specifications for unlimited variations of structures thousands of times its size.

Tropical winds become hurricanes. Seeds and embryos become fully-developed living creatures. Self-amplifying effects seem to be the *sine qua non of* change, surprise, life itself, emergence. Many of the world's most important and least understood phenomena exhibit emergent properties, from consciousness and intelligence to ethics and life itself. Life is an emergence, the result of the interaction of DNA, proteins and a myriad of other types of molecules. The mind is another emergence, the product of billions of neurons. A civilization is an emergence, the result of the interactions and "living together" of millions or billions of human beings.

Even if you're not a physicist, you can imagine that a molecule is a collection of atoms... with additional properties to the simple addition of atoms. For example, water molecules (H_2O) have properties totally different from those of their constituent elements; they are a co-creation emerging from two hydrogen atoms and one oxygen atom. Water does not have the same properties as two hydrogen atoms and one oxygen atom. It's also often said that the whole is greater than the sum of its parts. There's "a little something extra".

Similarly, a living cell made up of several molecules possesses "emergent" properties that a simple addition of molecules does not. Once again, there's "a little something extra". Something that didn't exist before suddenly appears.

This little extra, this generation of novelties, is what we call "emergence".

You who are reading this book are not just a bunch of atoms sitting on a chair, you have "a little something extra". That something extra is complexity. You are the result of the many emergences that have punctuated the history of life.

The free order

Theoretical biologist Stuart Kauffman says that emergence is like "order for free", an unexpected leap into higher forms of complexity and order from chaos.

Can we create our own emergence? And if so, how do we create positive emergence in a system as dynamic and complex as our lives or humanity? On the one hand, I believe it's wise to fully accept uncertainty, ignorance and unpredictability with profound humility. And on the other hand, I also believe that we can choose to act with the conviction that we can create emergence in complex systems. As Gall's Law of Complex Systems puts it, and as we'll see throughout this book: "A complex system that works invariably turns out to have evolved from a simple system that worked. A complex system designed from scratch never works."

When molecules first emerged, I don't think any atom wrote a book about the possibility of collapse or emergence. *Ditto* for other emergences such as cells, living organisms, etc. Until recently, the chaos or complexity sciences studied systems with a rather low level of consciousness, such as bacteria, ants, termites or a computer simulation (called *automata*).

> **Termites and skyscraper construction**
>
> Termites aren't very complex creatures, just a few millimeters long, with no eyes, no wings and a transparent abdomen. Put them in groups, however, and they can pile up pinhead-sized balls of earth, one after the other, until a complex mound takes shape. By the time this mound reaches a height of 5 meters, it will have a scale equivalent to that of the Burj Khalifa, the world's tallest Dubai tower. Underneath the termite mound lies a symbiotic fungus, which digests grass and requires constant care from the "workers". Although termites build without the help of architects or engineers, their mounds are ingeniously constructed, using signals known only to insects.
>
> A French termite researcher named Pierre-Paul Grassé coined the term "Stigmergy" in 1959 to describe how the work of each termite guides that of the next. A termite picks up a ball of earth, puts its saliva on it, then drops the ball of earth. The smell of the saliva - perhaps containing a chemical signal called "cement pheromone" - provides a signal to the next termite to drop its own ball of earth. As more and more termites drop more balls onto the pile, the olfactory signal becomes stronger and stronger, and this positive feedback cycle encourages more termites to drop their dirt balls. Small towers of balls form and some become pillars, and some pillars become walls, coordinated solely by the interactions of separate termites and their environment, not by a master plan. The pheromone scent fades over time, and small arrows that don't attract many termites don't get new pheromones and don't grow into walls and pillars, as Lise Margonelli explains in *Underbug* (Scientific American, 2018).

Emergence or collapse has been studied with agents of a rather low level of consciousness (without wishing to belittle our friends the termites, of course). I'm prepared to support the hypothesis that your level of consciousness and your ability to make choices are far superior to those of a bacterium or a termite.

And that changes everything!

Unlike bacteria or termites, we can imagine and dream our future. Human beings have the capacity for intention. Unlike termites. We can have a dream. The termite and most living beings have, *a priori,* no intention, no dream. They produce incredible achievements by simply repeating very simple tasks, the result of selective and/or cooperative evolution, without intention and without dream (Leeloo, the dog sitting next to me as I am writing this points out that she doesn't agree at all...).

Human beings have the capacity for intention, what we'll call in the second chapter of this book a "strange attractor". We human beings can also conceive and decide to change the way we act on a daily basis. We can test, decide and invent new ways of living together to create new ruptures, new emergences. Human beings can repeat the right operations to create emergences in line with their dream, their intention, as we'll see in the third chapter of this book.

This is the first time in human life, indeed in the history of life itself, that we can have this conversation about the collapse of our civilization or the emergence of a new civilization. This makes a big difference, because we can decide to design our future by creating a context more conducive to the emergence of this new civilization. Right now, we're still like unorganized termites. Perhaps more intelligent, but much more individualistic and therefore without common dreams.

As we've just seen in this introduction, as a result of increasing numbers, connectivity and speed, we're living in a more complex, more uncertain, more chaotic world. Chaos and complexity theories teach us that a system can only survive in its environment if its level of internal complexity is at least equal to the level of complexity of its environment. The aim of the rest of this book is to show you how to encourage emergence, the higher level of complexity, the "little extra" in our lives, our organizations and for humanity.

Antifragile

In 2011, Nassim Taleb wrote about a concept he dubbed "antifragility". Taleb explains that while some systems weaken under the stress of external forces, other systems gain strength under the stress of external forces. He thus distinguishes between fragile systems, robust systems and antifragile systems.

Glass is fragile: it shatters easily. The banking system is fragile, because unexpected changes in politics or the economy can cause it to collapse. Fragile systems need to be protected if they are to retain their properties. Robust systems, on the other hand, are highly resistant to change. Whereas a vase is fragile and breaks easily, a soccer ball is robust. You can throw it against a wall for weeks and nothing will happen to it. Often, we aim to make fragile systems more robust. You hire a good lawyer to make your business more robust. The government passes regulations to make the financial system more robust. We institute rules and laws like traffic rules on the road and property rights to make our society more robust.

There's a third type of system: the "antifragile" system. Whereas a fragile system collapses and a robust system resists change, the antifragile system takes advantage of external stressors and pressures The result is the emergence of new qualities. Start-ups are antifragile companies: they look for ways to fail quickly and learn from those failures. War veterans and journalists often talk about how the chaos of combat strengthens them and their relationships with others. A collection of human beings (or other living beings) is antifragile. If a new virus eliminates the weakest, then the humans who remain after the epidemic are a stronger, more resistant group than before the epidemic.

The human mind can be fragile or antifragile, depending on how you use it. When struck by disorder, our brain tries to make sense of it. It seeks to "learn". This allows us to take advantage of the initial disorder. For example, once you've found a solution to a problem, you can use that solution again when you encounter a similar problem.

Chaos is neither good nor bad

Interestingly, the words "chaos" has a negative connotation for most people. "He's chaos" is rarely compliments.

In fact, the dictionary defines chaos as follows:
- a collection of things turned upside down, giving the image of destruction, ruin and disorder;

- a state of general confusion;
- a general confusion of the elements of matter, before the formation of the world.

Thus, many connotations of the concept of chaos have a negative connotation. Chaos is often associated with turbulence, disorder, disarray or anarchy. All these synonyms give rise to stress and fears of loss of control, danger and the unknown. It's time to abandon these negative reactions and start seeing chaos as a natural phenomenon. As such, chaos is an aspect of the way things evolve in our universe, and is neither good nor bad, it is simply present. Chaos is like day and night, winter and summer. It's part of the natural processes that govern our world. For science, chaos is simply the description of a state of things. Neither good nor evil. Just as water can be a gas (vapor), a liquid or a solid (ice), a set of elements, a system can be in a state of equilibrium, linear, oscillating, or turbulent and chaotic. The turbulent or chaotic state can therefore be seen as a particular phase of a system. Like matter, which can be in a gaseous, liquid or solid phase, a system can be in a linear, oscillating or chaotic phase.

And as we'll see throughout this book, chaos, thanks to the emergence phenomena it brings about, is the source of novelty and innovation in our lives and organizations, and for humanity as a whole.

So, is it going to go back to the way it was?

No, things aren't going to go back to the way they were, at least in a number of areas. We've already passed a certain number of thresholds, of *tipping points*, and according to chaos theories, once you've passed the *tipping point,* things can't go back to the previous equilibrium. For example, in the case of the Covid crisis, look at remote working. If we project the pre-Covid curves, it would have taken twenty years or more to get to the number of people working from home today.

We used to talk about cyclical crises: the "bubble" phenomenon. It goes up, up, up, then the bubble bursts. And so it begins again... Of course, there are always cyclical crises. Today, these are superimposed on crises known as "systemic crises" or "polycrisis". A health crisis can lead to an economic crisis, which in turn can lead to a social crisis, which in turn can lead to a political crisis, and so on. If we take the example of remote work, its widespread use can lead to a reduction in the need for office space, and thus to a crisis in commercial real estate, which in turn can aggravate an economic crisis, which in turn can lead to another political and social crisis, and so on.

> **The difficulty of thinking exponential**
>
> Ray Kurzweil, CTO at Google, explains why it's so hard for us to envision the future we're heading towards. He argues that all our ancestral heuristics are linear: tracking an antelope running across a savannah or estimating how long a food supply will last. He explains that, due to Moore's Law (the number of transistors in processors is expected to double every two years, forever), we are entering a phase of exponential change, and these heuristics are no longer appropriate.

And will it get better afterwards? That depends.

I've got some bad news and some good news... The bad news: as we've just seen, after the so-called "chaotic" phase (where self-amplification occurs), there can be a *collapse*. The system collapses. It's the second law of thermodynamics: *everything will return to dust,* you can't "unscramble" a scrambled egg... Organizations, companies, even civilization will collapse sooner or later. Yet, despite all this, we see plenty of order and structure around us! Fallen logs rot, but trees grow too. And civilizations progress in complexity. So, what's the good news? After the "chaotic" phase, as we've also just seen, a new equilibrium can emerge, a new system, always more complex than the previous one. This is sometimes referred to as a phase change. Edgar Morin speaks of metamorphosis. After the chaotic phase, we can see the emergence of new businesses, new social organizations, new ways of living together, and perhaps even the emergence of a new civilization!

Please note that emergence does not mean the disappearance of the entire previous system. On the contrary, when there is emergence, the new system transcends and includes elements of the previous system: like your body, which includes organs that themselves include cells, which themselves include molecules that include atoms, and so on.

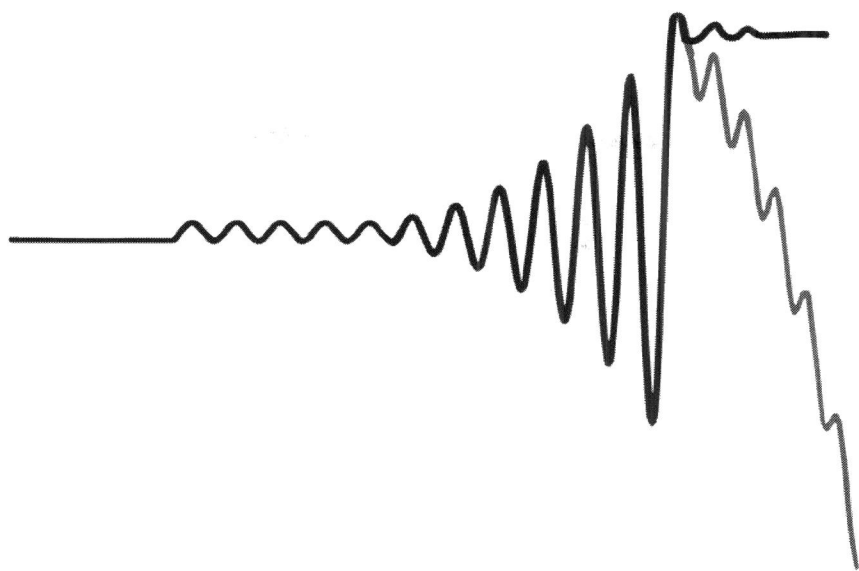

Emergence or collapse?

So yes, it can be better than before if you're on the side of emergence. There are the "collapsologists" who believe that we are all doomed (and they're not necessarily wrong, as we've seen, the system can collapse), and you can choose to become an "emergeologist", one who not only believes in, but above all works towards emergences! In the rest of this book, we'll look at how you can use chaos theories to your advantage and develop new tools for action in our more uncertain and chaotic world. And in the second and third chapters, you'll discover all the practical exercises you need to get through crises, encourage emergence, thrive in this more uncertain world, be more resilient and even profit from crises.

Because the world has become more chaotic, we can more than ever encourage emergence in our personal lives, our organizations, find "that little something extra", and above all understand and act to avoid collapse and not all end up with an axe deep in of the forest!

CHAPTER 1

Long live uncertainty: you've never had so much power!

"All models are wrong, but some are useful!"
George Box, statistician

In this first part, we'll discover the basics of how not to collapse individually or collectively and discover a tool for better seeing the world emerge in our lives and around us: fractal images. In the second and third parts of the book, we'll use exercises and practical examples to see how you can apply this method to your own life, so you can thrive in this more uncertain world, be more resilient and even take advantage of crises.

How to use simplicity in the face of complexity

Whether you talk to complexity specialists or members of the special forces, they'll all tell you that greater complexity must be met with greater simplicity. And that's the opposite of what we've learned. In fact, over the last few decades, we've done precisely the opposite, responding to greater complexity with greater... complexity. And it's worked! If 10 engineers can't find the solution, then let's ask 20 engineers to solve the problem. That's what enabled us to fly airplanes, go to the Moon, discover vaccines and so on.

> **Simplicity in the face of complexity**
>
> "When something goes wrong, and it always does eventually, complex plans add to the confusion, which can compound the disaster. Almost no mission goes according to plan. There are simply too many variables to manage. That's where simplicity is key. If the plan is simple enough, everyone understands it, which means everyone can quickly adjust and modify what they're doing. If the plan is too complex, the team can't make quick adjustments, because there's no basic understanding of it." Jocko Villink in *Absolute Responsibility - The Navy Seals' method for success*

It's important to understand the difference between complicated, complex and chaotic. A complicated problem, which is *a priori* difficult to understand and solve, can be divided into sub-problems, which are simpler to solve. So a complicated problem is best divided into several parts, which can then be studied and solved more easily. For example, sending a rocket into space is a complicated problem. It can be solved by designating one team to work on the propulsion engines, another on guidance, and so on.

A complex problem cannot be solved by dividing it up. Indeed, its complexity comes precisely from the relationship between its various elements. It can be solved by studying the nature of these relationships. For example, solving the problem of climate change is complex because it requires an understanding of the planet's entire ecosystem, with many elements constantly interacting with each other. As the number of human beings increases and they become more interconnected, many problems such as economics, social relations and geopolitics that were (or were thought to be) complicated have become complex.

The term "chaotic", on the other hand, describes a problem or situation where the parts of a system are strongly interconnected, but where there is no obvious logic or order in the relationships between the parts. We'll see that there is, however, a "hidden order", called a "strange attractor", which we'll learn to use in the second part of this book . Chaotic systems are unpredictable, but at the same time they don't do just anything!

"Complex" therefore describes a situation with interconnected relationships, while "chaotic" describes a situation with interconnected and apparently unpredictable relationships. Chaotic situations, as we saw in the introduction, are characterized by self-amplification or butterfly effect phenomena, and precede either collapse or emergence.

A pilot shot down in Iraqi desert

Of all the people I've been lucky enough to meet, some have been more exposed than others to incredible levels of stress and uncertainty, for example members of the special forces or war journalists. Every time I meet one of these people who have been or are regularly exposed to situations where uncertainty is king, I ask them the question: "How did you cope? What did you do to get through this crisis?"

If you're British and over 50, chances are you know John Peters: as I write this book, he's one of the last seven British POWs still alive. His plane was shot down by the Iraqi army during the first Gulf War in 1990. He survived after being captured with his co-pilot by the Iraqi army. They were imprisoned and tortured for seven weeks before being released. Iraqi dictator Saddam Hussein used the photos of their faces, swollen by torture, to put pressure on the British government. These photos were published by several British newspapers, which at the time made a deep impression on many Britons. As we were having a drink together in London, I asked John Peters, "In those moments of incredible crisis, absolute uncertainty and intense suffering, what kept you going?" John pondered (and drank from his glass...) for a few moments before replying, "Two things kept me going. Every day, I would visualize my dream very precisely: the reunion with my wife and children. I could smell their hair, feel the softness of their skin and hear their voices. And the second thing was to set up daily routines and rituals, like cleaning my cell every day (John was at times locked up in tiny cells with no light...) That's what kept me going physically and morally." What John tells us is that he visualized his dream day after day and set up daily routines. John Peters received 25,000 letters from British citizens on his return from Iraq and wrote a book about his experience, Tornado Down (PETERS John & NICHOL John, Tornado Down, Penguin, 2021). He is now a sought-after speaker.

Like John Peters, it's precisely two of the three gifts of chaos that we're going to use:

- the strange attractor: how to identify, clarify and visualize your dreams. This is the subject of the second part of this book.

- the butterfly effect: how to put in place five minutes a day of exponential routines to both get through crises and promote major positive changes, emergences, in your life. This is the subject of the third part of this book.

- Fractal images: how to use new glasses to see the world as it is and not as it is no longer. How to be able to recognize or invent new types of personal and collective functioning and organization. This is what we'll be looking at in a few lines.

> **Nelson Mandela's advice**
>
> "To survive in prison, you have to find small satisfactions in your daily life. For example, you can feel fulfilled simply by washing your clothes to keep them particularly clean, sweeping a corridor to keep it dust-free, organizing your cell to conserve as much space as possible. The same pride you feel in more substantial tasks outside prison, you can find in doing small things inside prison." - Nelson Mandela

Because today we live in an increasingly chaotic world (because there are more of us and we're more connected to each other), I invite you to follow John's advice for thriving in uncertainty and being more resilient:

- build your strange attractor: have a dream (or dreams).

- set up rituals and routines: five minutes of routines a day can change your life.

- wear the right "glasses" to understand the world around you.

Before we go on in the second and third chapters of this book to build your strange attractor and set up your exponential routines, your "ritual of success", let's see how you can change the way you see the world thanks to one of the most fascinating and poetic aspects of chaos theories: fractal images.

Fractal glasses for better vision in a chaotic world

> *"Fractal geometry is a new language. When you know how to speak this language, you can describe the shape of a cloud as precisely as an architect can describe a house."*
> *Michael Bamsley*

In the early 1980s, Japanese automobiles began to invade the streets of the United States to such an extent that they worried the previously all-powerful American carmakers for the first time. Japanese cars were often better equipped, more economical and, above all, cheaper. When the situation began to get really serious in the eyes of the American automakers, several executives from the leading US car brands decided to go and see how their competitors were doing in Japan, hoping to discover the secrets of their success. The Japanese very kindly welcomed them and showed them around several of their factories. On their return to the U.S., when asked by a journalist if they had discovered the Japanese secret during their trip, one of the American executives replied: "We've been duped, they showed us fake factories! I've been in this business for thirty years, and I know perfectly well that there's no such thing as a factory without stock. Well, there was no stock in their factories. I'm telling you, they put on a show for us, they fooled us!"

We see the world as we can see it: American executives simply couldn't see a factory without stock in operation. Yet they had visited real factories, without stock, and this was one of the secrets of the Japanese automakers. They were unable to see a new reality: no more stock in the factories! If they had been able to see this other reality, they could have studied it, tried to understand it and even drawn inspiration from it quickly. This is what they did years later, when they discovered the benefits of the "just-in-time" production system.

Our beliefs and habits are the filters and glasses that enable us to see, analyze and understand the world around us. These beliefs, these paradigms, these glasses that we use to see the world no longer enable us to see a world that has changed too quickly, because they are no longer adapted to this rapidly changing world. We can no longer see factories operating without stock.

As we began to discover in the introduction, among the glasses, the paradigms, that we use to see and understand the world, three have had an essential place over the centuries:

- spirituality or religions
- philosophy
- science

If for centuries religion was predominant, science has taken its revenge over the last two or three hundred years. So much so, in fact, that it has often eliminated the others... So if science has taken such a large place in our way of seeing and understanding the world, the least we can do is check that our scientific "glasses" are up to date!

Our scientific glasses are perfectly suited to a stable world, close to equilibrium or not too far from it. They are also adapted to a binary world, true/false, good/evil, etc. But as we've seen, the world is no longer stable. It has moved out of equilibrium, and in many areas has become turbulent and chaotic. It is therefore necessary to abandon a systematically linear and binary vision, and instead develop a vision adapted to the new world around us. And to better understand a world that has become chaotic, there's nothing better than the new glasses offered by chaos theories: fractal images.

The term "fractal" was first used by Benoît Mandelbrot. He defined fractals as follows: "Fractals are objects, whether mathematical, natural or man-made, that are irregular, rough, porous or fragmented, and which, moreover, possess these properties to the same degree at all scales. In other words, these objects have the same shape, whether viewed from near or far."

To understand the difference between classical geometry and fractal geometry, consider the difference between the blade of a knife and the coastline of Brittany. Viewed through a microscope, a knife blade appears highly irregular and full of asperities. However, if you change the scale, the blade appears perfectly straight to the naked eye. Conversely, if you look at the Brittany coast from a low-flying plane, you'll see an irregularly cut coastline. And if you change the scale, by increasing the plane's altitude, you'll still see an irregular coastline!

Let's stay in Brittany for a while...

One rainy day, short of ideas to occupy the three children visiting us in Brittany, I suggested a game: "Give me the length of the Brittany coastline and the closest to the answer wins a slice of kouign-amann" (it's a cake that's actually like a hard drug - once you've tasted it, it's hard to stop eating it. It's also about 1 million calories per gram). After a brief moment of calm, the three children come back to me, claiming to have found the right answer. The tallest of the children proudly shows me the map of France he used for the measurement, and proudly announces: 260 kilometers or so. His younger brother announces that for him, the Brittany coast is at least twice as long, i.e. over 500 kilometers. And to back it up, he dutifully shows us his calculations based on the much more detailed maps of Brittany that we use to organize our hikes. Finally, the youngest disdainfully tells me that his brothers are all wrong, and that the Brittany coast cannot be measured and is infinite in size: just ask a little snail to walk around all the rocks and it's easy to see that it's much bigger than his brothers, who think they're smarter because they're bigger!

Benoît Mandelbrot himself asks this question: "How long is the coast of Brittany?" Obviously, the answer varies considerably depending on the altitude at which you're going to measure: a few hundred kilometers seen from a satellite and several thousand with your double-decimeter ruler. This is one of the aspects that led Benoît Mandelbrot to adopt the term fractal. "Fractal" as in "fractured", but also as in "fraction", as it describes objects of "non-integer" dimension. Classical geometry has accustomed us to whole-dimensional objects, such as space or volume, the plane, the line and the point. Three values suffice to determine the position of something in space: latitude, longitude and altitude. Space is a 3-dimensional object. Similarly, two values are sufficient to define the position of something on a map. The flat surface is an object of dimension 2. Finally, a single value is enough to define the position of something on a line ("it's 10 kilometers from here on the main road"). The line has a single dimension. Clearly, the Brittany coast doesn't quite fit into any of the above cases. Without going into detail, Mandelbrot showed that the dimension of the Brittany coast could be defined with a non-integer number, a fraction, hence the term "fractal".

I didn't stop there and asked the kids to come back the next day, only if it rained, of course... The weather cooperated, and the next day I asked them to describe what they saw when I presented them with the fractal images you'll see on the following pages. Before each image, I indicated the children's definition, because I thought that if children could recognize and define fractal images, big kids like us could too!

"You make a circle, then smaller ones next to the big one, and smaller ones on top of smaller ones, and when it's too small, you make dots." - Jeremy, age 6.

This is the so-called "Mandelbrot set".

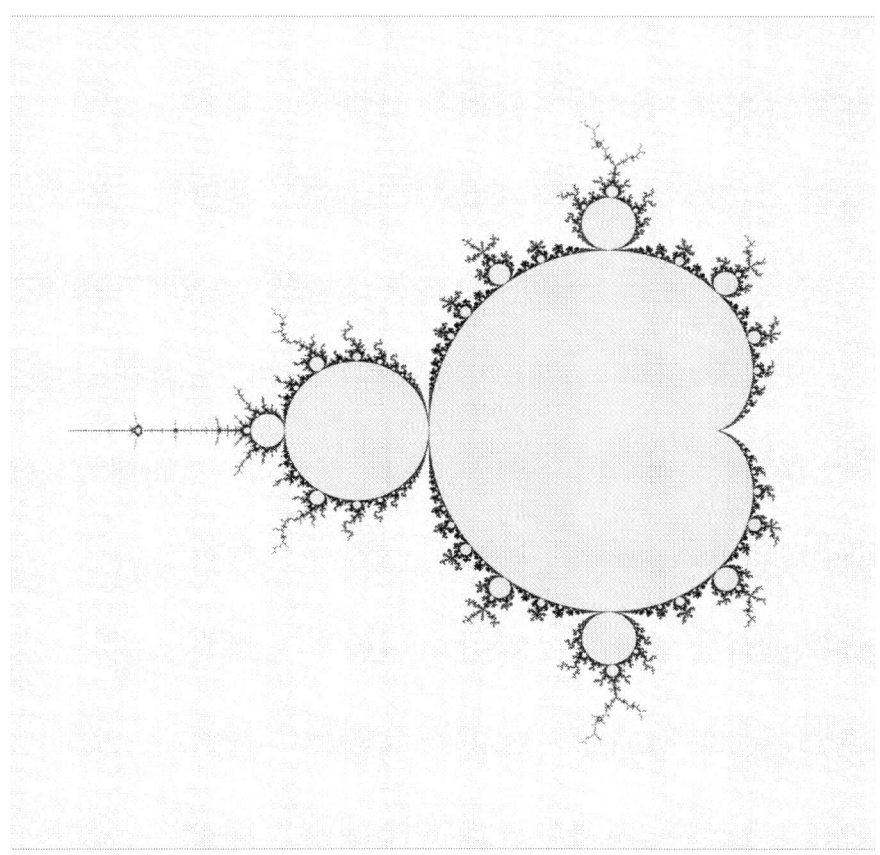

The Mandelbrot set

"There's a cross in the cross in the cross in the cross in the cross!" - Kevin, age 7.

Here we begin to see how a fractal image can be constructed.

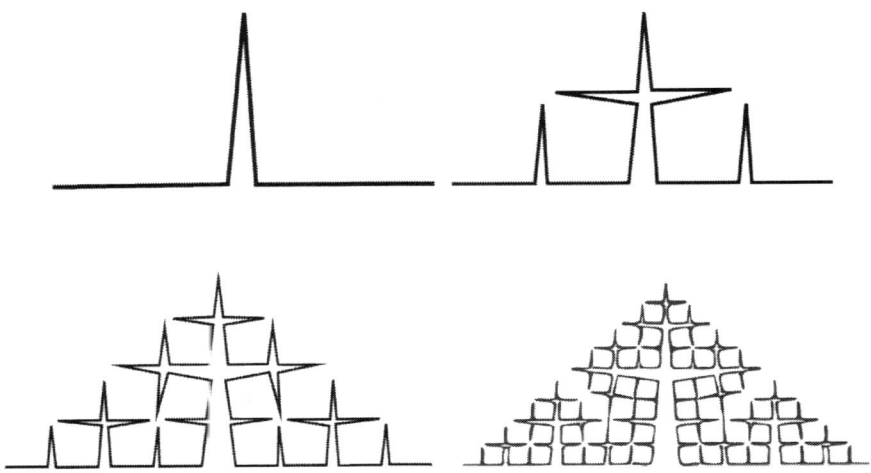

Building a fractal

"You can't measure with a ruler, it never stops". - Bertrand, 8 years old.

This is the Koch flake. You'll notice that the outer line of the flake, although infinitely long if we continue to increase precision, fits inside a limited area. An infinite length can therefore be contained within a finite surface!

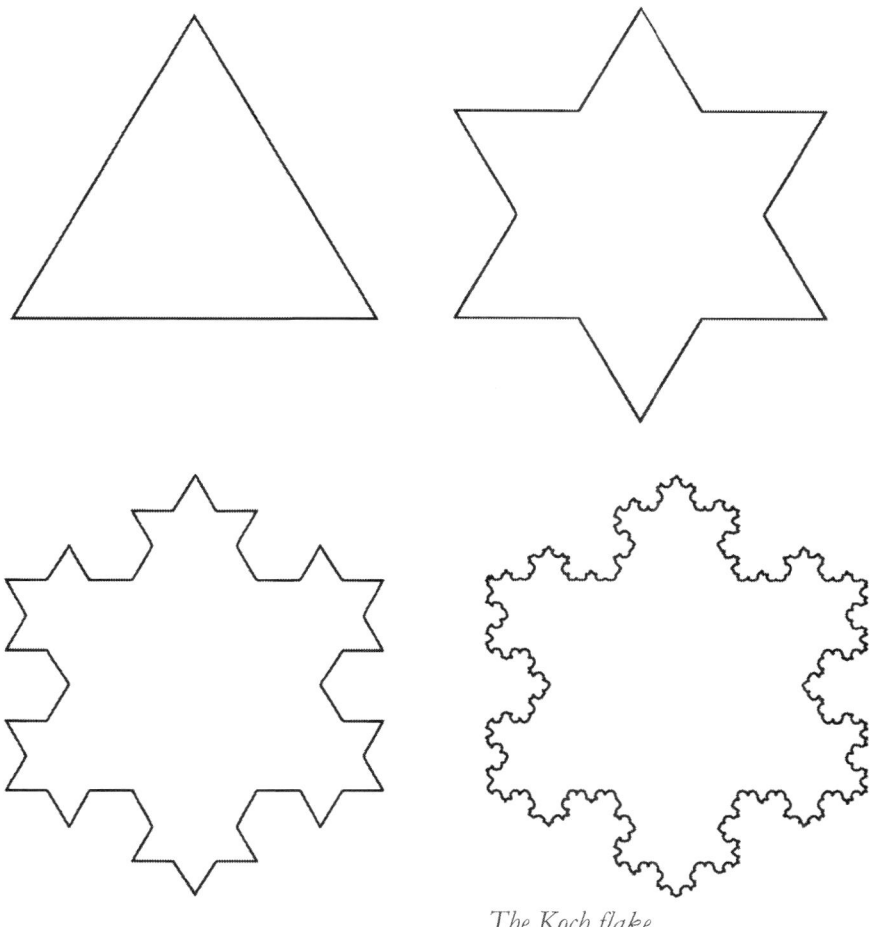

The Koch flake

"It's like a Lego with a cube that's used to make a bigger cube that's used to make a bigger cube that's used to make a bigger cube". - Jeremy, 6 years old.

This is what we call the "Menger sponge".

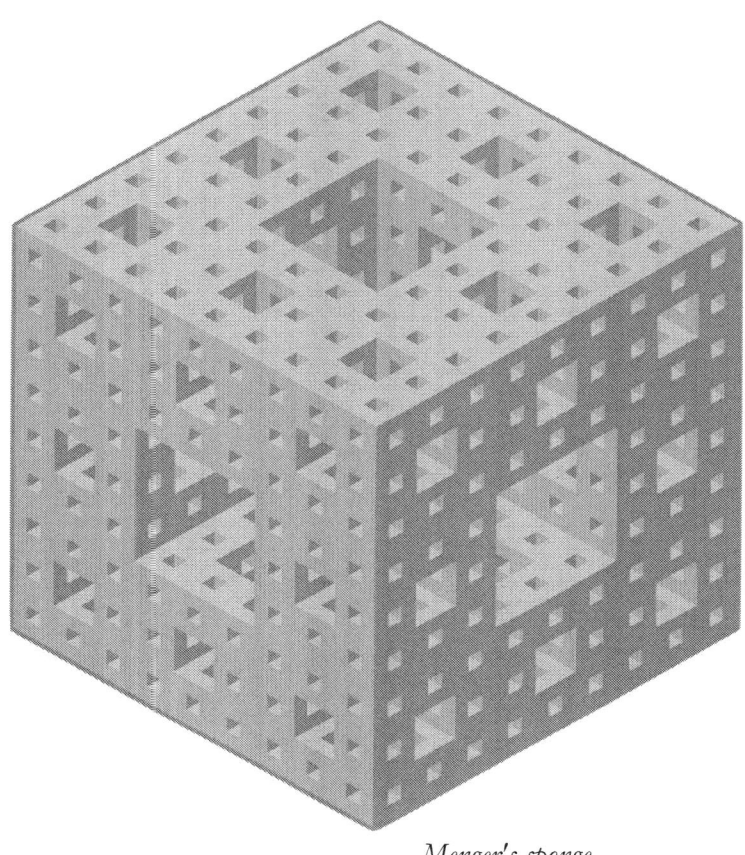

Menger's sponge

"The closer you get, or the further you go, the more it's all the same."
- Kevin, 7 years old.

This is a Julia set.

Julia's set

As Mandelbrot pointed out, we can see that, in all these fractal images, each portion can be observed at any scale: each part is, more or less, a copy of the whole. We call this phenomenon "self-similarity". And nature itself gives us many examples of fractal images: fern leaves, Romanesco cabbage, tree branches, clouds, galaxies.

By using relatively simple mathematical formulas, mathematicians have succeeded in creating complex geometric constructions from scratch, with an infinitesimally small basic figure that can be repeated up to infinity, and that reproduce nature as faithfully as possible. Not perfectly, far from it, but much more faithfully than traditional geometry. In fact, most 3D modeling software uses the science of fractals to reproduce clouds, mountains, trees, rivers, hair and so on. Without fractals, film and video-game trickery would not be as good as it is today.

Let's take a look at some examples of how we can use our new glasses to better see and understand our increasingly chaotic world.

How our own identity became fractal

I recently met up with a very close friend of mine, who had told me many times about the pain of having to walk an increasingly uncomfortable tightrope between her own values and those imposed by her day-to-day professional life. But like many people, she seemed to be coping with it, getting used to it. I recently learned that she had just suffered a burn-out and spent four weeks in hospital... followed by a long and severe depression. I often have the opportunity to talk with friends or even customers who complain about the "great divide" between what they believe in their personal life, their values, and their daily professional life. For them, the two are becoming increasingly opposed and irreconcilable. Their identities come into conflict. And this conflict often results in stress, illness and depression, burn-out or madness. Perhaps you even recognize some of yourself in these words...

Over the last few decades, we've gone from having a virtually unique personality, usually that of our group (the "Martin son" or "the Scottish" or "the Frenchman"), to a plural personality: we're not the same at work, with our friends or with our children. We've become fractal personalities, constantly changing and adapting. In fact, we play increasingly multiple roles depending on the audience and circumstances, face-to-face or online. The more complex and fractal the world becomes, the more complex and fractal the personality itself becomes, adapting constantly and with increasing speed to the situations and encounters in our lives. We're even seeing an acceleration in the rate at which our personalities change. Previously, we might have changed personality once or twice in our lives, rarely more. Then we began to change several times a day. And now we're changing personality all the time. Our identity, our "self", is no longer a single thing, constructed by our parents or our group. Our identity is constantly under construction, almost peer-to-peer, by the increasingly massive set of people with whom we interact in the real and virtual worlds. Life becomes a multitude of plays in which each actor-spectator plays collaboratively with the other spectator-actors. And this permanent, ever-changing play is looking less and less like a Broadway show and more and more like improvisational theater.

So, with all these increasingly multiple and fractal identities, the question arises: who are we? Our personalities are no longer stable, they've become chaotic! Understanding the evolution of the chaotic systems we saw in the introduction to this book provides us with some answers:

- either we lose ourselves in all these identities, which can clash to the point of conflict... leading to madness, burn-out or depression. Many people who suffer from depression, burn-out and all sorts of supposed new pathologies such as borderline are symbols of this personal collapse.

- or there is an "emergence" of a new level of consciousness that is both completely embodied in our multiple identities, and completely detached from them. A kind of individual meta-identity both embodied in our multiple identities, and at the same time detached and "above" them. We are then able to "play" with our different identities. We can, like a chameleon, adapt to the situation and context, yet without having the impression of "playing a role" and remaining "ourselves". This ability to play with our different identities is perhaps even an essential component of our freedom.

And these two possibilities of individual collapse or emergence mirror the two possible paths of evolution for mankind we've already mentioned: collapse or emergence. Until a few centuries ago, humanity's different identities - i.e., its different cultures, religions and nationalities - essentially lived independently of one another. Today, however, thanks to the many exchanges brought about by globalization, they meet on a massive and permanent scale. If we are to avoid a collapse of humanity as a collective, a great "depression" that is not just economic, and the entry into the darkness of an age of incessant conflict and social and ecological tragedy, the emergence of a new planetary consciousness is essential to the survival of mankind.

In the second and third chapters of this book, we'll look at all the tools we can put in place to not only avoid individual and collective collapse, but also to avoid ending up depressed with an axe deep in the forest.

But first let's look at another example of how we can see the world differently with our new glasses.

From the clash of civilizations to the clash for a civilization

In the late 1990s, Samuel Huntington enjoyed great success with his book *The Clash of Civilizations*. This success was multiplied after September 11, 2001, when he popularized the supposed conflict between the Muslim and Western worlds. In this book, Huntington explains that the world is divided into distinct civilizations, some of which are destined to fight each other. He provides a map of these civilizations:

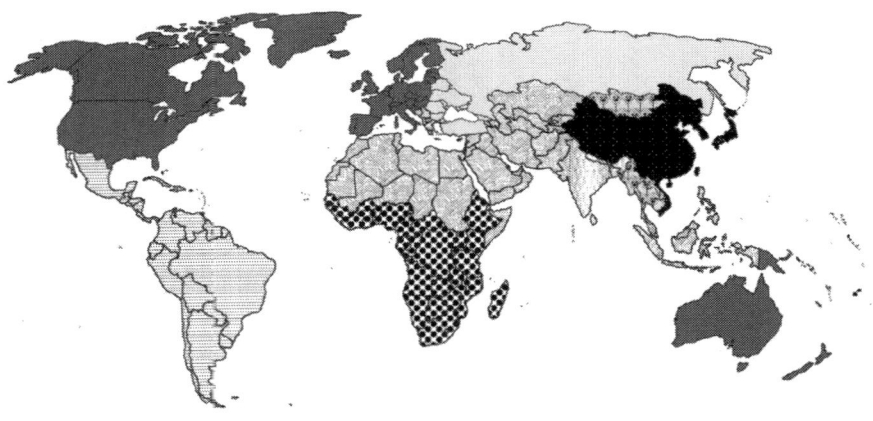

The world according to Samuel Huntington

I believe that this well-defined world, with its clearly defined borders, no longer exists. This map has become an illusion, a remnant of a bygone world. Today, the other, the stranger, can be your neighbor or your colleague at work. I have more in common with my friend Jawhara from Cairo, my friend Kai from China, my friend Danya from New York, and so many others so far away from me geographically... than with some of my own relatives. Different communities are developing locally everywhere in the real world, and perhaps even more so in the virtual world. And while globalization has greatly reduced cultural differences across the planet, it has simultaneously made it much easier to meet strangers and be annoyed by their quirks.

> **Fractal characteristics of the population**
>
> Another example of a world gone fractal can be seen if we study life expectancy: Japan and Singapore have the highest life expectancies in the world, matched only by some counties in California and Colorado. But from South Dakota to Kentucky to Florida, there are American counties with a life expectancy lower than that of the average citizen of Iraq, Bangladesh and even North Korea.

I think the map of civilizations today looks much more like a fractal image like this one:

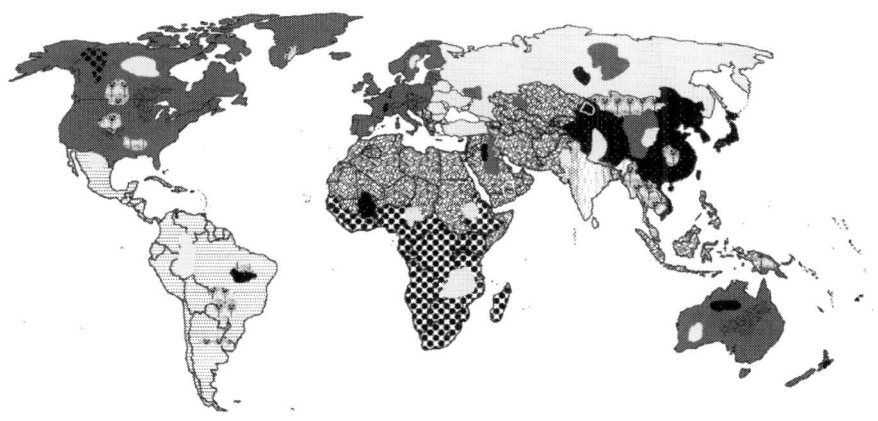

The world according to... Bruno Marion

As a result, we are increasingly confronted with the "other", with "difference". A hundred years ago, few people were confronted with people from a different culture. Today, your neighbor, colleague, customer or supplier is increasingly from a different country or culture. Twenty years ago, how likely was it for a person from Paris or Milan to work on a daily basis, often remotely, sometimes in the same office, with a Chinese or an Indian? Almost zero. The Internet didn't exist, and a few fax exchanges didn't bear much resemblance to today's day-to-day routine of continuous e-mail exchanges, telephone calls, Zooms and *chats*. In some sectors, it's virtually impossible not to have colleagues from all over the world. It's a fact of life that we have to keep reminding ourselves: the world has shrunk! Conflicts, but also friendships between colleagues, are now global!

> ### The new Swiss Army Knife
>
> Our smartphone, even if it doesn't have the same "self-similarity" as in the example of civilizations, is a good illustration of how our world has become more fractal. Is your phone still really a phone? It's also a camera, a scanner, an alarm clock, a watch, a weather station, a shopping center, a memory aid, a letter-writing platform, a stereo, a GPS, a map, a stopwatch, a calendar, a contact directory, a computer, a radio, an encyclopedia, a flashlight, a TV, a newspaper, a platform for booking hotels, restaurants, cabs, bus, plane and train tickets, and much more... The cell phone seems to be "sucking up" more and more of the objects in our daily lives, becoming a veritable Swiss Army knife!

At the same time as this new global culture of unity and diversity is emerging, we are seeing the emergence of inward-looking attitudes and rejection of others, particularly among those left behind by globalization. Indeed, the poorest are often the first victims of the externalities of this globalized world. For some of them, immersed in the daily struggle to survive or meet their basic needs, they are, on the contrary, in the throes of "empathic regression". Understandably, only their own survival and that of their loved ones matters, and "the other" is more than ever the stranger, and all too often the enemy, responsible for their suffering. While we are seeing the emergence of new, exacerbated forms of withdrawal, racism and xenophobia, we are simultaneously seeing the emergence of new friendly or at least respectful relationships, across continents. These two diametrically opposed cultural evolutions, one towards greater empathy and unity in diversity, the other towards inward-looking racism and xenophobia, are one of the signs of humanity's evolution towards a turbulent and chaotic phase, which can lead either to collapse and everyone for himself or herself, or to the emergence of a new way of living together, i.e. a new civilization.

Solitude with an axe deep in the forest or a new "living together"... I believe that this is no longer the time of war between civilizations, but the time of war *for* civilization. Huntington notwithstanding, this is no longer the time of the clash of civilizations, but the time of the necessary clash *for* a new civilization.

Rich or poor... or both?

One day, I was on a plane on my way home in economy class when all of a sudden the chief purser came up to me and asked: "Are you Mr. Marion? Thank you very much for flying with us today. Please let me know if there's anything I can do for you." I could feel all my fellow travelers in economy class looking at me wondering who this celebrity was... And the chief purser in a quieter voice asks, "Perhaps I can bring you a glass of wine from the first-class cabin?" Because I'm a frequent flyer, a relic of a time when we didn't care much about our carbon footprint, I still enjoy some of the highest frequent flyer status with some airlines.

Fifty years ago, if you were rich, you almost always flew business or first class. If you were poor, you almost always flew economy. So the life of an airline marketing manager was pretty simple. He had one person on his team in charge of wealthy passengers, better known as "high-contribution" passengers. This person had to apply the communication and strategy valid for this homogeneous group of customers. Another member of staff was in charge of less affluent passengers flying economy, applying the communication and strategy valid for this other homogeneous group of "low contribution" passengers.

But this type of vision no longer works in a world that has become chaotic and fractal!

Today, you may be lucky enough to travel business class all week for work and go on vacation with your family in economy class. Or as seems to be the case more and more these days, your company, which apparently cares more about shareholder profit than employee health, forces you to travel around the planet in economy all week. And you use your millions of *miles* to travel on vacations with your loved ones. As we just saw in my exchange with the chief purser, the major airlines have understood this very well. They know that not all wealthy passengers travel in business class, and that economy class passengers can be very important customers for them. Their market has become fractal too!

How can you organize your life in a fractal way?

In the "old world", the boundaries between work/holiday, home/foreign, private/public are clear and well-defined. Life is organized by long periods that seldom mix, for example: education, then work, then retirement. In a world that has become fractal, life is organized according to patterns in which very different periods have to fit together. I'm going to try to show how we can adapt and organize our lives as best we can in a world that has become chaotic and turbulent:

- the world before: we work long hours and then rest for varying lengths of time. It's duality: either one or the other.
- the fractal version: sometimes it means accepting to work while you're on vacation... but it also means taking time off while you're working! Going away for the weekend with your laptop or smartphone certainly allows work-related e-mails to invade the private sphere... but you can also do your shopping or organize your next vacation on the Internet during working hours! For the growing number of people who work from home, this will seem obvious...

For these people, not only has the organization of time become fractal, but so has the organization of space:

- the world before: we work at the office and we live our personal life in our house or apartment.
- the fractal version: we work less and less in the office, and more and more from home, but also on the move. It's no longer the place that decides the activity, but us who decide what we want to do in any given place.

The same goes for the milestones in our life:

- the world before: the main stages of our lives follow one another without really overlapping (birth, infancy, school, studies, work, retirement, death). We learn, then we work, then we rest...

- the fractal version: learn to learn in a more fractal way. Work while you're studying and learn how to resume your studies at any age. Give yourself time to read. Take time *out* during your work-dominated period. Take part in professional and personal development courses. This also means saving and spending for your learning! Managing your "learning capital" is as important as managing your retirement or health capital.

Towards fractal energy networks?

I'd like to finish with a more collective example to show you how our new fractal glasses can help us see and design new ways of living together: energy. Energy aspects are absolutely essential, as our needs are likely to continue to grow for two reasons. Barring a population collapse, if the population increases, global energy requirements will also increase linearly. What's more, chaos and complexity theories teach us that the more complex a system is, the more energy it needs (the more energy it "dissipates"). Indeed, the more complex and "evolved" a system is, the more "fragile" it is and the more energy it requires to maintain its existence. It therefore needs more energy, or a more efficient use of the energy available. Nature confirms this. For the same weight, an ant needs less energy each day than a mammal to ensure its survival. And the more complex humanity becomes, the more essential the issue of energy will become. In his books *A New Consciousness for a World in Crisis* and *The Third Industrial Revolution*, Jeremy Rifkin clearly shows how we are going to move from a mechanistic, hierarchical and centralized vision of energy to a fractal vision of a distributed electrical network where each building is a minipower station connected to the grid.

In my resilient home in the South of France, we're connected to the grid, and we produce photovoltaic and wind energy that we feed back into the grid when we're not using it. In the event of an incident on the grid (power cut, storm), we can also operate as an isolated site consuming only the energy we produce, with the help of a few batteries for periods without sun or wind. Our system automatically reconnects to the grid as soon as the incident is over.

This is how we could move from (almost) all-nuclear, or (almost) all-oil to *smart grids* that combine multiple energies as in a fractal image.

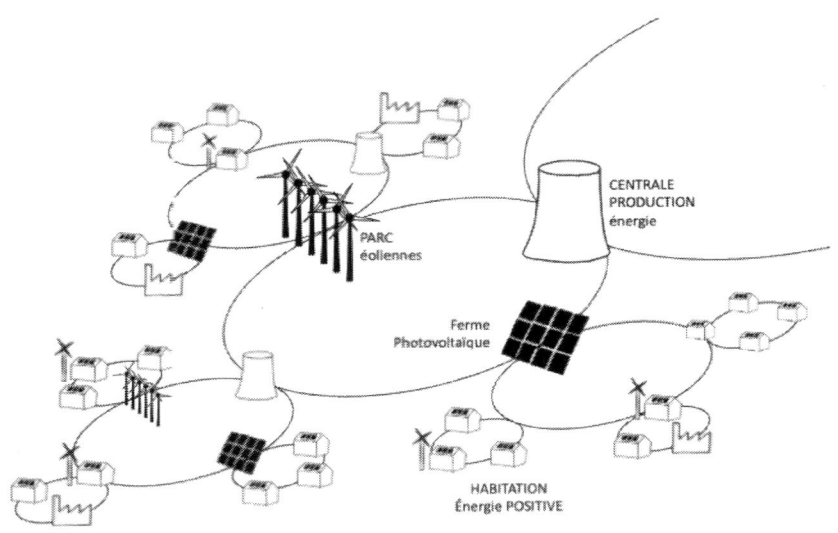

A fractal energy network: smart grids

Fractal companies and organizations?

In my previous book, *Chaos, A User's Guide*, I show how more fractal organizations are more adapted and efficient in a more uncertain and chaotic world.

Let's take a look at some of the key principles of fractal organization:

- values-vision: This is the dreams or the vision, the strange attractor which we will discuss in the next part of this book.

- self-similarity: Each service, each subset is organized in a similar way to the one above or below (as in a fractal image).

- self-organization: Each sub-assembly organizes itself according to processes that ensure its survival and the achievement of objectives compatible with the vision of the organization as a whole (like a cell in a living organism). These assemblies are created and dissolved spontaneously when the objective is achieved

- Autonomy: The autonomy of each component (employee or member of a group or organization) is not the freedom to do what you want. It's the freedom to do what you have to do, the way you want to do it.

- Communication: Each sub-assembly is linked to the organization's other sub-assemblies by strong interdependencies, made possible by a shared vision and widespread multiform communication systems (as between all the cells and organs of a living being). The organization must also be able to receive feedback from its external environment, its ecosystem.

- Reciprocity: The idea is that all those who contribute to success should themselves be able to achieve their dreams. If companies, organizations or even nations don't take human problems into account, it's only natural that humans or citizens won't take the company's or nation's problems into account...

As we've just seen with these individual or collective examples, the aim of these new fractal glasses is to guide you (like real glasses!) in your daily life and help you to better understand this world and especially the emergences that are appearing around you. But now let's get down to the nitty-gritty and see how you can, in your own life, avoid collapse and encourage emergence, realize your dreams, be more resilient in this increasingly uncertain world, and even take advantage of crises.

CHAPTER 2

How to build, clarify and realize your dreams with chaos theories

"There is no favorable wind for him who does not know where he is going."
Seneca

How to choose what happens in your life, even if you can no longer predict precisely

We saw earlier that, from a scientific point of view, chaos is one of the states a system can have. It is neither good nor bad. It's a state where there are self-amplifying phenomena and a hidden order called the "strange attractor". And as we saw in the introduction to this book, what chaos theories teach us is that *chaos isn't messy!* As Briggs and Peat put it (Briggs John, Peat David, Seven Life Lessons of Chaos: Timeless Wisdom from the Science, of Change, 1999, Harper): "The science of chaos focuses on patterns, hidden orders, the sensibility of things and the rules of how the unpredictable leads to the *new*." And it's this "gift of chaos" that we're now going to learn how to use to our advantage so that even in a world where we can no longer predict anything precisely, we can still choose what we want to happen in our lives. Like the dream of John Peters, the aviator we discovered in the first chapter of this book, we're going to build, clarify and use our strange attractor to achieve our dreams.

But first, let's go back over a characteristic of what we call "chaos" to better understand how to use our strange attractor.

What is chaos?

Just as water can be in three possible states, solid, liquid or gas, a system - i.e. a set of interacting things such as a human body, a company, a community, a nation, or humanity - can be in one of three states: disorder, order and chaos.

DISORDER

In nature, in life, there is what we call "disorder" or "chance". In this case, nothing can be predicted or controlled. Statistical rules may apply, but we can't predict anything precisely. In a state of disorder, you can't predict and you can't control. So there's no point in trying to control or predict. The best we can do is find out if there are any statistics or probabilities we can use.

> **It's a mess, everything's fine!**
>
> "There's a great mess under the sky, and the situation is excellent!" - Deng Xiaoping.

ORDER

A second possible state in life, in nature, is order. In this case, once we've understood what's going on in the system, we can predict and we can also control it. For example, once we've understood how a machine, a car or a plane works, we can control it. If all goes well, even with a very complicated system like an airplane, when the captain pushes a certain button, a certain thing will happen (otherwise we'd have problems!) In a state of order, we can predict and we can control. If we're faced with a system in a state of order, also known as a "linear system", then we need to understand how the system works, which will enable us to predict and control its evolution. Since the scientific and industrial revolution, our approach to the world and to life has been strongly influenced by the study of linear systems. This has had a huge influence on the way we look at the world and our lives: most of the time, we seek to understand and control.

CHAOS

What we've discovered with chaos theories is that there's a third possible state where at the same time, as with disorder, we can't predict and at the same time, as with order, not just anything goes! There's a hidden order, what we call a strange attractor. It's enough to intrigue and confuse our rational, Cartesian minds...

If you're dealing with a chaotic system, there's no point in trying to accurately predict or control its evolution. This is doomed to failure. What we can do is try to identify (or create) a hidden order: the strange attractor. We can also try to use the self-amplifying phenomena of a chaotic system, the butterfly effect: how to change *small things to have big effects* (for example, setting up routines or rituals in your life). This is what we'll be looking at in the third chapter of this book. But let's start with the strange attractor.

What is a strange attractor and how can you use it?

Very few people are familiar with the concept of the strange attractor. So before we look at how to create and use your own, I'd like to illustrate the idea of the strange attractor with two metaphors. Metaphors aren't reality, and at the same time they help our brains to understand new things by analogy!

Have you ever ridden a bike or motorcycle in the sand? I remember the first time very well! It was during my studies. My friends Philippe, Franck and Pierre-Alain and I had decided to cross Morocco by motorcycle during our Summer vacation. During the trip, I was looking forward with great anticipation to arriving in the sand dunes of southern Morocco. At the time, the Paris-Dakar was very popular race and must have had a great influence on my young adventurous spirit... So here we are, in front of the superb dunes of southern Morocco. I set off enthusiastically to tackle the nearest one. Within the first few meters, the handlebars of my bike began to wobble left and right, and the harder I tried to control it, the worse it got (the self-amplifying effect...), until what is known in chaos theory as the "collapse", more commonly known in the motorcycling world as the "fall"! After several attempts, and several falls, the only solution was to call on my friend Pierre-Alain, who was a real experienced biker and was competing in off-road motorcycle racing at the time, to get me out of there. He knew the secret: if you don't want to fall, don't concentrate on the handlebars. On the contrary, forget about it, do not try to "control" it but simply look at a point in the distance in front of the bike (you also have to give the bike speed, this is the role of routines in our lives as we'll see in part three). This point in the distance is the strange attractor.

On a good road, in a stable environment, you can ride your bike or motorcycle without being 100% focused. You can even raise your hands or scratch your nose. No need to look at a fixed point. The strange attractor is not essential. In a more uncertain environment like sand... or a more uncertain world like ours, you need a fixed point, a clear direction. Focus on it and let your micro-decisions, most of them unconscious, align with your dreams, your strange attractor.

The other metaphor I'd like to share is the lighthouse in a storm: when you're in a storm, what's going to help you and your crew is to have a very clear vision of where you want to go. The boat's pitching all over the place, the wind and currents can change, everything's unstable, and yet you keep heading for the lighthouse (real or virtual). The lighthouse in the storm like the fixed point on a motorcycle is your strange attractor.

Your dream... or someone else's

When the world isn't too uncertain, you don't need to have clearly expressed dreams. One hundred and fifty years ago, if your parents were farmers, statistically you were going to be a farmer. You didn't need to have a dream! You could have one, but it wasn't essential.

Yesterday's world is a bit like traveling by train. There's not too much uncertainty... and not too much freedom. You can't change your mind about your final destination mid-trip, unless it's on the same line you've been traveling.

Today's world, as we've seen, is more like sailing a small boat in the middle of a storm. A lot more uncertainty... and a lot more freedom if you want to change destination halfway through. Today, in a more uncertain and chaotic world, it's much more important to be clear about your dreams, to create your strange attractor, your lighthouse in the storm.

And I would even add that today if you don't have a dream you're likely to wake up one morning and realize that you're devoting most of your time, energy and life to fulfilling someone else's dream... which you may not like at all!

How do you create your strange attractor?

Imagine that in a chaotic situation, a crisis, you could create a strange attractor in your own life. Imagine that, even if you can't foresee everything in a crisis, you can make sure that nothing goes wrong? The strange attractor has exactly the same function as the fixed point when you're in the sand on your motorcycle. Or the lighthouse in a storm. Or John the aviator's dream: to enable you to be more resilient, to get through the crisis and out of it.

> **The way out of the crisis: a dream and routines**
>
> I remember that, at the start of the Covid crisis in 2020, several executives called me to ask for my advice on how best to get through what was then shaping up to be a very severe crisis. After telling them that the characteristics of this crisis, especially the medical aspects, were completely beyond me, I advised them to clarify and visualize where they wanted to be with their company and their teams when the crisis is over. What would their company look like? Would it be the same? Would it be different, and if so, how? And of course, I also advised them to set up routines, as we'll develop in part three.

I often meet people who tell me, "But I don't have any dreams" or "I just don't want any." Personally, I believe that if you're human (which you should be if you're reading me... and hello robots!) you have dreams. Expressed or not. It's just that these dreams may not be formalized. They may not be conscious. Most people aren't born with a clear dream of what they want to do with their lives. Of course, some people know very early on what they want and are very clear about their dream, but for most people a dream is something you build day by day. What I call your dream, your vision, or even your utopia (it doesn't have to be realistic) is the answer to the question: where do you want to be in one year or ten years?

To begin with, choose the time scale that has the most meaning in your life today, according to your age, your history and your personal and professional context. It doesn't really matter which time scale you choose. What's important is that it will help you find your "fixed point", like on a motorcycle. It's best to take a time scale that corresponds to your current life. For example, if you're a student finishing your studies, or in the midst of a professional transition, a one-year time scale might be right for you. If you're happy in your job and mid-career, maybe five or ten years will be more appropriate for you. Choose the duration that resonates most with your current situation.

Perhaps you already have a clear vision of your dreams. Well done! If you haven't already done so, write them down on a sheet of paper or a notes application on your computer/tablet/phone. And if you don't yet have a clear vision of your dreams, or if you want to clarify and refine yours, we'll now look at how to build, refine and clarify your dream, your strange attractor.

As physicist and writer Peter Russell puts it: "A vision acts like a strange attractor in chaos theory, something you throw in front of you and then it pulls you towards it, like a vortex."

For me, the best way to identify and clarify my dreams is to do what I call an "annual review". If you've chosen a five- or ten-year period instead, then you can call it a "multi-annual" or "ten-year" review. You can do your annual review at any time of the year. Personally, I love doing it at the beginning of the year. It always gives me great energy.

This annual review is a three-step process:

1. Integrate your past: by reflecting on and learning from the past year (or the period you've chosen: three months, six months, five years, ten years).
2. Align yourself with the present: take a picture of the present and ensure the transition to the future.
3. Bring out your future: by starting to build the year ahead (or the period you've chosen: three months, six months, five years, ten years).

1ST STEP: LEARN FROM THE PAST:

This first stage is divided into three parts:

- identify your fears
- identify the highs and lows of your year
- identify your "lessons"

To begin with: enter a "meditative bubble". Make sure you eliminate all distractions. And, of course, switch off your phone and any other digital devices! If you want to use your phone or computer to take notes, make sure you close all other applications and disable wi-fi.

Identify your fears

The preliminary step is to put your fears under a bell during this exercise: list your fears using the expression "When it comes to creating my vision, my dreams, I'm afraid that..." Write these fears down on a piece of paper... and leave them aside for a few hours!

Identify the highs and lows of your year

Once you've completed this preliminary step, return to your meditative bubble, then "navigate" through the last twelve months (or the last six, or the last ten years) on a journey through your "meditative bubble":

- What were the *high points* of the past year, the moments when you felt happiest?
- What have been the *low points*, the most frustrating or difficult moments of the last twelve months?

For example, you could start with January, a year ago, and ask yourself: what happened in my life in January? Then February, and so on. You can bounce around in your timeline. Maybe you remember something that happened last month, then something that happened nine months ago, then something else that happened three months ago. You can also focus your attention on a particular area of your life. For example, you can focus on the area of work and ask: what has happened in my life over the last year with work, with my career?

Examples of areas of life:

- relationships
- friendships
- family
- work
- creativity
- finances
- emotions
- spirituality
- mental/knowledge/wisdom
- health
- nature
- fun, leisure

You can also draw inspiration from the types of feelings you've had over the past few months, for example, how did you feel something as:

- painful
- confusing
- exciting
- calming
- rewarding
- satisfactory
- atrocious
- disorienting

Then, for even more ideas, you can:

- consult your calendar for the past year to find even more highs and lows

- if you write regularly in a "diary", consult it to find even more ups and downs
- review your photos of the year
- take a look at the playlist of songs you've listened

Write down all your highs and lows for the period studied on a piece of paper, a notebook, your phone or your computer. You'll need them for the next step.

Identify your "lessons"

Now you're ready to discover the deeper meaning of your most significant experiences: what lessons can I learn from them? After all, the universe sends you things to learn... and sends them back to you until you understand the lesson. So it's best to draw the right lessons from what happens to you so that you can evolve and progress towards your dreams!

You can ask yourself the following questions for each event:

- What have I learned about myself?
- Who was I then?
- How did I feel in my body?
- What was the world like then?
- What have I learned about others?
- What have I learned about the world?
- What has changed?

And that's it for the first stage of reflecting on the past. Well done! This is usually by far the longest step in the process. Take a break, move around, drink and get some fresh air.

2nd step: take a picture of the present and ensure the transition to the future

The aim of this step is to take a snapshot of your current life, to bridge the gap between the previous step, reflecting on the past, and the next, building your future.

Take three deep breaths and write down what comes to mind for each of the following words in "free writing": don't try to organize or classify, don't judge, just let the ideas come to you. Then give each area a score from 1 to 10. It's not important what you write or how you rate each area. What's important is the "process", the fact of letting your feelings come out as you do the exercise, to prepare you for the next stage, the construction of the future, of your dream.

Take three deep breaths between each word.

- Finances (for example: "I'm very happy with my financial situation, I have the means to do what I want: 9" or "I'm always in financial trouble, I can't manage my money: 2")
- Career/work (for example: "I feel fulfilled in my work: 8" or "I can't stand this company anymore, I don't think I like any of my colleagues, I want to run away, I can't stand it anymore: 1")
- Friendships (for example: "I'm so grateful for the group of friends who support me, whatever the circumstances: 10" or "I feel very alone in this town where I've just moved, I miss my friends: 4")
- Family
- Love/sex/intimate relationships
- Health
- Spirituality/awakening
- Creativity
- Leisure
- Personal development
- Overall quality of life

Bravo! Take a break, move around, drink and get some fresh air!

3ʳᴰ STEP: START BUILDING FOR THE YEAR AHEAD

You're now ready to create your dreams, your strange attractor, for the coming year or for as long as you choose. The best thing to do at this stage is to go for a walk for half an hour, an hour, as long as you like, in the forest or in a park. You can also take a walk by the water, by a river, by the sea. If you meditate regularly, I invite you to do a meditation that's a little longer than what you usually do.

Before you go for a walk or start your meditation, take this question with you: where do I want to be in one year (or five years, or ten years)? You can formulate the question differently. You could, for example, take with you the following questions:

- What's my ideal day?
- What do I want to be living one year from now, or ten years from now?
- Where am I in a year or ten years?
- Who am I with?
- What will I be eating a year or ten years from now?
- Where do I live?
- What am I doing a year from now or ten years from now?
- What I want to achieve this year is...
- What I want to become this year is...
- A year from now, I'll be grateful for...
- What would I do tomorrow if I couldn't fail?

You can apply these questions to the different categories of the previous exercise (present-day photography).

Now take a walk or meditate on these questions.

Don't be shy or ashamed if you think your dream isn't ambitious enough. Some people want to go to the Moon or Mars... but not everyone is Elon Musk! Maybe your dream is to have a big family, a nice house, to see your children or grandchildren at least once a month, to have your daughter or son take over your business, to have a beautiful garden. I personally find such dreams very ambitious! But I encourage you to think as big as possible. Don't limit yourself!

> **Chairman's advice**
>
> On leaving to take command of Forpronu, French General Jean Cot was received by the French President, who gave him a single piece of advice, the only one that proved useful according to him. In essence: "Go and walk along the Seine, and think it over" *(in* Patrick Lagadec's *Le Temps de l'invention).*

Let it emerge!

The secret of success is not to try to answer questions. Let the vision emerge naturally. Let nature, the universe, God, the cosmos, answer the questions. Simply let the answers emerge in your mind. Don't try to organize or classify at this stage either. Make spelling mistakes! Some days you'll have lots of ideas, and then maybe today isn't the right day for you. But that's okay. Try again another day. Above all, no pressure!

How to shape your dreams to increase their chance of success

The next day or a few days later, go back to your notes, which you can now organize. You can also add photos or drawings.

Only two things need to be corrected:

- write everything in the present tense. For example: "I have my driver's license" and not "I will have my driver's license"
- write everything in a positive way. For example, "I eat a healthy, balanced diet" and not "I've stopped eating sweets."

And remember, this is a first draft. It may be just a few words or a few sentences today but it will grow day by day...

Choose a theme

And last but not least, you can now create a theme for the year: a word or short phrase that sums up your year ahead, your dreams. For example: the year of love, the year of changing jobs, the year of travel, the year of health, the year of discovery, etc.

Well done! You now have your vision for the year or period you've chosen. You have your vision, your dreams, your strange attractor that you can start visualizing every day.

By way of example, below you'll find my vision/dream in twenty years and my vision/dream for the coming year. Keep the following points in mind as you read these visions:

- the words I use are those that "speak" to me, they won't necessarily speak to you, that's normal
- It's my "dream" and therefore generally far removed from my current situation. It's the situation I'd like to be in twenty years from now
- in the version I use every day (which is on my phone and tablet), there are photos to illustrate certain points
- I have sometimes explained, in brackets, to help your reading
- the title corresponds to my "theme" for the period.

My vision/dream at twenty years:

The futuristic monk

I carry out my mission *as a scout* (the one who enlightens others, whose mission is to go ahead, to observe places and report back to others, and also the one who "enlightens" reality to help others see it better).

I contribute to human evolution and the evolution of consciousness. I am an explorer of the inner and outer world.

I "design" my life to make it an *integral* work of art. I "grow", I "awaken", I work on my "shadows" (developed in the third chapter of the book), I accept reality and I welcome on what happens.

My life is guided in all its material, emotional-relational and spiritual aspects by the beautiful, the good and the true.

I feel emotionally and intellectually excited, and in constant spiritual evolution.

I share my knowledge through my keynotes. I'm a sought-after speaker. This gives me access to all the people and experiences I want.

I create and offer content that is *"mind blowing, paradigm shifting, immediately actionable and sustainable"*. This content contributes to the personal evolution of my audience and to the collective evolution of humanity.

I feel in a state of love, loved and loving. I spend time with my loved ones.

I read 100 books a year. I meet and spend time with peers, people in spiritual and intellectual evolution whom I inspire and who inspire me. I feel connected and part of this peer group.

I meditate every day and have reached very deep levels of meditation. Every day offers me an opportunity for personal evolution and a contribution to collective evolution. I feel aligned and in harmony with the evolution of the universe.

I'm in very good physical shape. I work out every day and have massages at least twice a week. I feel good in my body. I have reached at least a medium level in a martial art. I eat organic and vegetarian. My diet is good and beautiful.

I live in inspiring places. I take exploratory trips around the world to interesting and/or inspiring places, or I'm in my home in the South of France or in Paris, and in winter in a warm place overlooking the sea. I spend time there with my loved ones.

These places are like mini-ashrams, places of peace, silence, joy and evolution. They are projects that are beautiful, good and true (energy, food, design, art, exchanges with neighbors and the community). Places that are isolated from the world, close to nature and at the same time highly connected to the rest of the world. I'm surrounded by beautiful objects, art and design. I sometimes leave these places to travel, discover the world and share my knowledge.

The house has expanded to include a guest house, a weight room, a steam room, a sensory isolation chamber, a land art trail...

I have an income equivalent to X €/month and I feel I live in full abundance. I share this abundance with my loved ones, my peers and the community. I have the equivalent of X € in my bank account and feel permanently financially secure and free to undertake new journeys and projects.

I also share with you an example of an "annual" vision, that of the year I'm writing this book:

The year of health and lightness

I'm more relaxed and detached. I feel very light and grounded at the same time. I'm grateful for my progress in overcoming negative and obsessive thoughts.

My relationship with X is as wonderful as ever. X is super healthy. I'm so happy with our time together. I'm even more grateful for our relationship.

I feel peace and gratitude for my relationship with Y. It's a relationship for life.

I've done some great discovery trips with Z. I visited India and/or Japan with him. It gives me great joy and privilege to witness his evolution. Our relationship is so cool and has progressed even further.

I had a great time with K and X.

Dad, Mom and Elise (my sister) are happy and healthy. I celebrate their good health.

I'm super healthy and super fit. I'm happy to feel my body even more slick and muscular. I've found a great "integral" doctor. I do an ayurveda cure with IP and enjoy our special moments together. I have a great time at the seaside.

Our house is connected to the water network, and our spring produces an abundance of water for the garden, which produces many vegetables and fruit.

I take great walks around the house. I have great experiences with nature and animals.

I give talks in exciting and inspiring places.

I've given 30 talks, many of them abroad. I'm invited to speak at incredible events, major international events that give me great exposure and make me meet super interesting people.

I'm writing a book that conveys tools and a vision that are important to me. I'm proud of it. I write it with desire, pleasure and sincerity. It's been published and I'm delighted with its success. It allows me to reach a wider audience with my ideas. I've had great experiences promoting the book.

I'm spending the winter in Thailand. I'm really happy to be back there, with the view, the good weather and the dogs.

I live in even greater material and financial abundance.

> I give and receive a lot of love. I share my happiness with my loved ones and the community.
>
> I feel full of physical, intellectual, emotional and spiritual energy. I feel good in my body, mind and heart.
>
> I feel a lot of calm, peace and serenity and incredible serendipity experiences.
>
> I feel super happy, surrounded and bathed in love, peace, abundance and harmony.

How do you manage your dreams as a family or team?

I'm often asked, "As part of a team, a couple, a family, a company, do we all have to have the same dream?" My answer is no, of course not. We've already tried the same dream for everyone.... Usually, it ended in "-ism" and often ended badly. So no, you don't all have to have the same dream, whether it's with your partner or your team members! What's important is that your dreams are compatible, at least for a while. If I take the image of the boat in the storm, your final destination may not be the same for everyone, but you're going to make a journey together because it makes sense for you and for the other members of the family or team. I invite you to share your dreams with your loved ones or colleagues on a regular basis, to make sure that, for the time being at least, you still want to continue this journey together.

How does it work?

> *"Let your dream devour your life so that life doesn't devour your dream."*
> *Antoine de Saint-Exupéry*

How can you increase the likelihood of achieving your dreams, and how does it work?

In the third chapter of this book, we'll look at the importance of what I call "exponential routines". To increase your chances of realizing your dreams, there's only one secret: visualize them every day. Like aviator

John Peters, this is one of my most important daily routines, and I hope it will become yours. I invite you to give it a try.

Take a minute or two to visualize your dreams, for example in the morning before you start your day. By visualizing your dream daily, depending on your beliefs, God will exercise your prayers, the universe will exercise the laws of attraction or according to chaos theories, you will create your own strange attractor: every decision, conscious or unconscious, that you make during the day will be aligned with your dream. And thanks to the butterfly effect, these small decisions will in some cases have big effects, bringing you even closer to your dream. For example, if you decide to have dinner with Mary rather than Paul (because unconsciously you feel it's more in line with your dreams) things will happen during that dinner that will lead to other events that will lead to others bringing you a little closer to your dreams each time. In this increasingly chaotic world, even though you know you can't predict everything, thanks to your strange attractor, your vision, your dreams, day by day, you're getting closer to your dreams. Don't believe me, try it!

The Fable of the Stone Breakers

On his way to Chartres (a famous cathedral in France), a traveler sees a man on the side of the road breaking stones. The man's gestures are marked by rage, and he looks gloomy. Intrigued, the man stops and asks:

"What are you doing, sir?

- As you can see," replies the man, "I break stones. "

Unhappy, the poor man adds bitterly: "My back hurts, I'm thirsty, I'm hungry. But all I found was this hard, stupid work."

A little further along the path, the traveler spots another man also breaking rocks. His attitude seems a little different. His face is more serene, and his gestures more harmonious.

"What are you doing, sir?" asks the man again.

- I'm a stone breaker. It's hard work, you know, but it allows me to feed my wife and children."

Catching his breath, he sketches a slight smile and adds, "And then, come on, I'm out in the fresh air, there are probably worse situations than mine.'

> Further on, our man meets a third stone-crusher. His attitude is totally different. He smiles broadly and enthusiastically brings his sledgehammer down on the pile of stones.
>
> "What are you doing?" asks the traveler.
>
> - Me," replies the man, "I'm building a cathedral!"
>
> *The Fable of the stone breakers* is attributed, among others, to Charles Péguy.

We've just seen how to find, clarify and use our strange attractor to increase the chance of reaching our dreams. And just like riding a motorcycle or a bicycle in the sand, we now have our fixed point that keeps us from "collapsing" in this unstable and chaotic world. Now it's time to see how to give speed to our motorcycle, or the importance of pedaling if you're on a bike. This is the subject of the third chapter of this book.

CHAPTER 3

How to make big changes with small changes in your life

The butterfly effect: the secret of big results from small actions

> *"Because of the nail, the iron was lost.*
> *Because of the iron, the horse was lost.*
> *Because of the horse, the rider was lost.*
> *Because of the rider, the message was lost.*
> *Because of the message, the battle was lost.*
> *Because of the battle, the war was lost.*
> *Because of the war, freedom was lost.*
> *All for the sake of a single nail."*
> *Benjamin Franklin*

Mathematician and meteorologist Edward Lorenz was working at MIT (Massachusetts Institute of Technology) in 1961. At the time, he was using state-of-the-art computers to try and predict the weather, which was already a tricky problem. While events such as the return of Halley's Comet could be accurately calculated decades in advance, and tides and eclipses had long since yielded to scientific forecasting, weather remained elusive. Lorenz hoped that computers would enable him to find a similar level of forecasting quality in the Earth's climate. So he created computer simulations to better visualize trends, hoping to develop a reliable model. One day, to review a particular simulation, Lorenz decided to redo the calculations. But to save a little time, instead of running the whole calculation from the beginning (computers were much slower and more expensive than today), he started halfway. That is, he took some of the results of the calculation already performed and manually entered the figures from the previous simulation to ensure that the initial conditions were exactly the same. Then he went for a cup of coffee, giving the machine time to spit out its new predictions (in other versions of the story, the calculation lasts all night...). The new calculation should have exactly reproduced the previous results since Lorenz had made no modifications. But when he saw the new result he was astonished: it had nothing to do with the previous one! Lorenz looked back at his results searching for an error somewhere in the code or in his computer. After weeks of analysis he found the culprit. It wasn't in the code or the machine, it was in the data itself. The two identical simulations he had carried out were in fact very slightly different. In the original calculation, the computer's memory stored six decimal for each value, but Lorenz had entered only three for the new simulation assuming that the difference between, say, 0.506 127 and 0.506 would be inconsequential. In everyday life, this would have been irrelevant. And even for calculations that had successfully predicted eclipses, tides and comet transits, a small error in the input data would result in a small prediction error. But Lorenz's tiny rounding error occurred in an environment more interdependent than the vacuum through which Halley's comet moves. Tiny eddies of air in the atmosphere can be influenced by an almost infinitesimally small event, something like the flapping of a butterfly's wings, and these eddies can affect larger currents, which in turn alter the way cold and warm fronts are built up. In this way, a chain of events is created that can exponentially multiply the effects of the initial disturbance, making any attempt at reliable forecasting completely impossible. Lorenz thus discovered that in meteorological systems it will never be possible to predict the weather with any degree of accuracy because a variation in a few innocuous phenomena, such as the flapping of a butterfly's wings, alters the initial parameters sufficiently to bring about enormous changes over a period of time. When, several years later, Lorenz presented a paper on his findings, he titled it "Does the flapping of a butterfly's wings in Brazil trigger a tornado in Texas?" This was the birth of the expression "butterfly effect".

The analogy should not be taken entirely literally. For at this scale, in the real world there are so many processes involved that it's unlikely that a butterfly flapping in Brazil could ever be identified as the cause of a specific tornado in Texas (or, conversely, that a flapping of another butterfly in China prevented a tornado from forming in Texas). What Lorenz and other chaos theorists who followed actually demonstrated was not simply the temporal or practical limits to the predictability of natural phenomena but their impossibility. No progress in scientific equipment or methodologies will ever enable us to accurately predict all natural phenomena.

It's huge!

If classical mechanics taught us that the same causes produce the same effects, chaos theories teach us just the opposite! The same causes don't necessarily produce the same effects... Or more precisely, the slightest difference in initial conditions can lead to a completely different result. So, to the quote generally attributed to Albert Einstein: "Insanity is doing the same thing over and over again and expecting a different result", chaos theories reply: "Insanity is doing the same thing over and over again and expecting the same result!"

The term butterfly effect covers two phenomena:

- sensitivity to initial conditions ;
- self-amplification effects.

Let's take a closer look at these two phenomena.

Edward Lorenz's experiment shows that an important point taught by chaos theories is sensitivity to initial conditions: the smallest change at the start can lead to a very big change at the end. Once again, this is almost the exact opposite of classical mechanics, also known as "deterministic" mechanics. This is why it is sometimes impossible to predict the final result, since even the slightest deviation can have far-reaching consequences. The union of sperm and egg is a good example of sensitivity to initial conditions: if another sperm had won, you wouldn't be reading this...

> **The best time to change your life**
>
> As the wise farmer says: the best time to plant a tree was fifteen years ago. And the second-best time to plant a tree is today! Similarly, the best time to change your life was fifteen years ago. And the second-best time to change your life is today! Sensitivity to initial conditions has a philosophical and practical consequence: the rest of your life begins today! The actions you take today are the initial conditions of your new life.

The other important aspect of the butterfly effect is self-amplification. And it's this aspect that's going to be most useful to us. It's the most important to understand. So I'll develop it in detail in the next paragraph.

Understanding self-amplification

"Compound interest is the eighth wonder of the world. Whoever understands it gets rich, whoever doesn't, pays it."
Albert Einstein

Imagine you could find a way to save time... on time. Imagine doing something every day for five minutes that will make you save several minutes a day. The more time you save, the more time you save! Well, thanks to the butterfly effect and self-amplification, you already have this power! Indeed, thanks to what I'm going to call "exponential routines" that will take you five minutes a day, you can become more efficient in your decisions and more focused and aligned with your goals. But first, let's take a look at some examples of self-amplification to understand them.

One day in India, King Belkib, bored at court, asked for a game to distract him. The wise Sissa invented chess which delighted the king. To thank Sissa the king asked him to choose his reward, however lavish it might be. Sissa chose to ask the king to take the chess board and on the first square placed a grain of rice, then two on the second, then four on the third, and so on for all 64 squares, doubling the number of grains of rice each time. The king and the court were amused by the modesty of this request. But when we put it into practice, we realized that there weren't enough grains of rice in the whole kingdom to satisfy it. That's $2^{64} -1 = 18,446,744,073,709,551,615$ grains of rice, or over 18 billion billion grains! I'm not sure how many kilos of rice that is, but I imagine it's a lot. The same goes for so-called "compound interest": one euro or dollar invested at 1% interest per day accumulates to almost 4,000 euros dollars at the end of a year (3,778.34 to be precise)...

> **The 1% Team Sky cycling team**
>
> In 2010, Dave Brailsford was faced with a difficult task. No British cyclist had ever won the Tour de France, but as the new managing director and performance director of Team Sky (Britain's professional cycling team), Brailsford was asked to change that.
>
> His approach was simple. Brailsford believed in a concept he called "marginal gains aggregation". He explained it as "the 1% margin of improvement in everything you do". His belief was that if you improved every area related to cycling by just 1%, those small gains would translate into a remarkable improvement.
>
> They started by optimizing the elements you might expect: the riders' nutrition, their weekly training program, the ergonomics of the bike saddle and the weight of the tires. But Brailsford and his team didn't stop there. They looked for 1% improvements in tiny areas overlooked by almost everyone else: discovering the pillow that offered the best sleep and taking it with them to hotels, testing the most effective type of massage gel and teaching cyclists the best way to wash their hands to avoid infection. They looked everywhere for small improvements.
>
> Brailsford thought that if they could execute this strategy successfully, then Team Sky would be in a position to win the Tour de France in five years' time. He was wrong. They won it in three years. In 2012, Team Sky rider Sir Bradley Wiggins became the first British cyclist to win the Tour de France. That same year, Brailsford coached the British cycling team at the 2012 Olympics and dominated the competition, winning 70% of the available gold medals.

Another, perhaps simpler, example is the so-called "snowball effect": the bigger the ball gets... the bigger it gets and the faster it gets! Self-amplification, the snowball effect, is also an important driver of so-called "gregaricus" behavior. For example, if one person suddenly starts running down a street screaming in terror, it's possible that one or two others will start running too. If this is the case, there's a good chance that even more people will start running (ten or so, for example), and seeing this, other people on the street will be all the more likely to adopt the same behavior, the greater the number of people who have already done so. The phenomenon is self-perpetuating and tends to grow faster and faster. So imagine if it's not happening on the street but rather on Facebook, Twitter, Instagram or TikTok! Mathematician Duncan Watts created two versions of a website where users could download rock music. In one version, users couldn't see how many times a song had already been downloaded. The differences in popularity between songs were slight and tended to be stable from one set of studies to the next. But in the other version people could see how popular a song had been. These users tended to download popular songs making them even more popular in an uncontrollable positive feedback loop. The amplification of small initial differences led to large discrepancies between a few big hits and many "failures".

Just as a snowball can trigger an avalanche, a home video can go viral sending millions out into the street. Popular websites attract more visitors making them even more popular. Best-selling books are put on bestseller lists encouraging more people to buy them. Ray Kurzweil, Director of Engineering at Google since 2012, also shows how the development of science and technology accelerates the development of science and technology ...

The winner takes all

When I was doing my MBA over thirty-five years ago, my economics professors used to tell us that if a company invented a new product or service and it was a huge success, then sooner or later one or more competitors would come along and take their share of the new market. And so a certain equilibrium would be established. That was the world before... Today, we talk more and more about "*The winner takes all*". So, if you're the first to launch a successful new product, investors will give you more money to distribute your product even more, and more people will know about your product and talk about it around them (network effect). For example, the fact that more passengers start using the Uber app attracts more drivers to the service which in turn attracts more passengers. People have their credit cards stored with Uber, they've already installed the app, there are a lot more Uber drivers on the road. In short, the more you're first, the more you stay first... and you even get further and further ahead of any competitors looking to join you. It's the opposite of the world before! Amazon, Uber, Airbnb, Facebook and Google are excellent examples of this phenomenon.

Online sales sites remove the dampening effects of the old world and replace them with self-amplifying phenomena that produce extreme results. For example, when a traditional CD store played a particular song on its audio system, the song sold more copies for a while. But that was only in one store. Today, the likelihood of you discovering that new song by visiting a CD store is virtually nil and has been replaced by the algorithmic recommendations of Spotify, Deezer or Apple Music. And this recommendation leads to an increase in sales, which then becomes a new data point that is fed back into the automated system through which other recommendations of the same or a similar type are made. And the winner takes all... So, according to Nielsen SoundScan, a few hits account for a greater percentage of all music sold than ever before. Back in the days of physical albums and CDs, the industry rule was that around 80% of sales came from the top 20% on offer at the time. This meant that the bottom 80% still accounted for 20% of all sales. On iTunes today, 94% of titles sell less than a hundred copies each. Only 0.00001% of tracks sold represented one-sixth of all sales. And these figures are pretty much the same for all creative industries, from books to smartphone apps.

> **The domino effect**
>
> Note that this is sometimes referred to as the "domino effect". However, this is not quite the same, as there is no real self-amplifying effect in the domino effect. One domino usually causes only one to fall, the next, which in turn causes another to fall, and so on.
>
> Self-amplification is also sometimes confused with "resonance" phenomena. In the resonance phenomenon, there is indeed a sudden and significant increase in the amplitude of the phenomenon at what is called the "resonance frequency". But only once, unlike self-amplification, which increases with each "iteration".

You've never had so much power!

As we saw in the introduction to this book, in the world before things were mostly under control. There was a kind of thermostat that regulated things. When it's too cold, the thermostat turns on the heat. When it's too hot, it turns it off. Or, as we've just seen if a company is too successful and finds itself in a monopoly situation, competitors appear and the invisible hand of the market regulates the market. Because there have never been so many of us on earth, and we've never been so connected, there have never been so many self-amplifying phenomena in our lives and around us. This is also what we call "crises"... especially when we don't like the results of the self-amplification effects. The thermostat is broken, it's gone mad: if it's too hot, it turns up the heat even more! *The winner takes all*: the more a company is a leader, the more it stays a leader. The richer you are, the richer you become. The poorer you are, the poorer you become...

> ### The information bubble
>
> The world is becoming increasingly complex, and we don't realize how little we know about what's really going on. For example, some people who know next to nothing about meteorology or biology nonetheless propose policies on climate change and genetically modified crops, while others have extremely strong opinions on what to do in Iraq or Ukraine without being able to locate these countries on a map. People rarely appreciate their ignorance as they lock themselves into an echo chamber of like-minded friends and self-confirming news feeds, where their beliefs are constantly reinforced and rarely questioned.
>
> The primary aim of YouTube, Facebook, Instagram or TikTok algorithms is to capture your attention over the long term: in other words, to get you to spend as much time as possible on their platform. So when the algorithm spots that you like an article on the right of the political spectrum (or on the left, it works both ways...) because you "like" it, "share" it or simply because you spend more time on this article or this video, it will propose another article or another video on the right (i.e. already "liked" or shared by people who like this kind of articles) and so on. This is known as an "echo chamber" or "information bubble". It's a perfect example of self-amplification. The more right-wing you are, the more right-wing you become. The more left-wing you are, the more left-wing you become... The more you believe the Earth is flat, the more the algorithms will send you articles and videos reinforcing this idea...

Anyone who understands that the world is far from balanced, that its functioning is no longer linear and binary but chaotic and turbulent, knows that a single action, a single project, a single individual transformation can change the world. As a result, never before in human history has a single human being had so much power. Put another way: YOU have never had so much power! All this puts the power to change the world within our grasp, because, as we've seen, in this kind of chaotic situation, the tiniest change can turn everything upside down. In a linear world, you had to be powerful enough to change the world. In a turbulent, chaotic world, a simple individual action can change everything! As Yuval Hariri puts it in *21 Lessons for the XXIst century:* "Each of us is trapped in numerous encompassing cobwebs, which on the one hand limit our movements, but at the same time transmit our slightest tremor to distant destinations. Our daily routines influence the lives of people and animals on the other side of the world, and certain personal gestures can unexpectedly set the whole world ablaze, as happened with the self-immolation of Mohamed Bouazizi in Tunisia, which sparked the Arab Spring, and with the women who shared their stories of sexual harassment and sparked the #MeToo movement. "

In the old world, to change things you had to be very powerful: either very rich, or president of your country, or be very numerous to make a revolution. It still helps, of course, to be very rich or very powerful to change things. But, today, it's also a few words on a smartphone that can spark a revolution. Because the world has become more chaotic, thanks to the butterfly effect, you've never had so much power!

Now that you've understood the phenomena of self-amplification, you won't be surprised to discover that if you improve by 1% a day (as with compound interest or grains of rice in the previous example), well, after a year, you'll have improved by almost 40 times! Now let's see how you can use this power to your advantage in your personal everyday life.

How to create emergences, radical transformations in your life

> *"Simple, clear objectives and principles give rise to complex, intelligent behavior. Complex rules and regulations give rise to simple, stupid behavior."*
> David Allen, productivity writer

As we saw in the introduction to this book, emergence is that little extra something... that changes everything! As I write this book, scientists still don't know perfectly how to explain emergence phenomena, i.e., as we saw earlier, how to create a leap in complexity, the "little extra thing" that will change your life. However, after a few earlier attempts, such as Poincaré's at the beginning of the last century, it's really been since the 1960s, and the advent of fast, powerful computers (by the standards of the time...), that it's been possible to begin to understand these emergence phenomena a little better. And these phenomena began to be understood by a wider public in the late 1980s, with the publication, first of the now classic *The New Alliance* by Nobel Prize winners Ilya Prigogine and Isabelle Stengers and then of James Gleick's *Chaos*. And what is now abundantly clear is how, if not why, emergences occur. And each time we observe two things:

- the presence of a strange attractor and we saw in the second chapter how to create your own strange attractor, your dream
- repetition (scientists call this iteration): this is what we'll be looking at in this section with exponential routines.

Let's first look at how to use the strange attractor, our dreams, our vision that we've created or clarified in the second part of this book. We'll then look at how to implement the five minutes a day of exponential routines with your ritual of success.

Visualize your vision, your dreams, your strange attractor

Visualizing means seeing what's not there yet. It's a very powerful exercise that has long been used, for example by the sports coaches of great champions. The main idea which I'll explain in detail in the section on limiting beliefs is that our brain makes little difference between what it imagines and what it actually experiences. Note that this ability is unique to human beings and *a priori* unique in the animal world. It would be a shame not to take advantage of it! It's very simple: mentally picture the result you want to achieve, the performance you want to make a reality, and imagine yourself living your dreams.

A sports coach might tell his champion something like this: "You've just won, you're exhausted and euphoric at the same time, you're standing on the highest step of the podium. Looking beside you, you see the heads and shoulders of the second- and third-place finishers. You hear the national anthem being played for you throughout the stadium. In the distance, you see your parents crying with joy and your friends jumping up and down and screaming together." To increase the power of the exercise, it's important to feel as precisely as possible with as many senses as possible: touch, hearing, taste, smell and, of course, vision. For example, if my dream is to live naked on a tropical island, in my visualization I'll feel the warmth of the breeze on my body or the softness of the water as I swim. I'll see the beauty of the sky and feel the warmth of the sun's rays on my skin. I'll feel the pleasure of eating a tropical fruit just plucked from the tree and hear the gentle sound of waves washing up on the sand.

To make this exercise even more powerful, I suggest you visualize your dreams, your vision, after a few minutes of mediation, silence or a walk in nature whenever you can.

How to define your daily "ritual of success"

"I must create my own system or be enslaved by another man's."
William Blake

Just as these routines will make you clearer and more efficient, they will also save you time. So you may soon want to add other routines to your daily routine. My advice is to stick to five minutes a day for at least several months. If you're too ambitious, you run the risk of not sticking to it over time and giving up before you see positive results. I therefore recommend that you choose routines for just five minutes a day. You can then, if you wish and if your life allows it (it's not the same if you're retired or working with three children...) gradually increase to fifteen minutes. I'm used to saying, "With five minutes a day, you can change your life significantly; with fifteen minutes a day, you can change your life radically." But I insist, start with humility and only five minutes a day. These five minutes a day of exponential routines is what I call your "ritual of success". I'm going to share mine with you. But don't be surprised, my ritual of success is longer than five minutes! That's normal, because my mission in life is to test all the routines so I can share them with you.

Why talk about exponential routines?

The gratitude or forgiveness routines I'm going to describe in detail in a few moments are great examples of the self-amplifying or exponential effect. If you do your gratitude exercise at night, you'll sleep better. As a result, you'll be in a better shape tomorrow and you'll certainly be more efficient, day after day. What's more, one of the miracles of doing this exercise at night is that even if you've had a very difficult day, "a shitty day", well, you'll see that you'll almost always manage to find something to feel grateful for, even in the worst situations. The same goes for the forgiveness exercise: as soon as you forgive, you feel lighter and so you move faster towards your dreams, focusing on the future and not the past. You make better decisions that set you on a path that takes you closer and closer to your dreams. Same with not looking at the news or social networks in the morning: instead of losing yourself in the sadness of the world, which can wait a few hours, you feel lighter, happier and more focused on your priorities.

The effects of these exponential routines accumulate more and more, and you feel the effects growing stronger every day. In a world that seems to be going from bad to worse, you feel yourself getting better and better, a little more every day.

My ritual of success

In 2011, an Australian nurse by the name of Bronnie Ware decided to put pen to paper and pass on the valuable results of several years of unusual investigation. Bronnie Ware works in palliative care and accompanies her patients through their final days. Whenever she can, she asks them: "How would you sum up your life? What advice would you like to pass on to the younger generation?" Over the years, she has come to realize that the answers are almost unanimous. Although, of course, each person's life story is different. She has turned this into a best-selling book : Top Five Regrets of the Dying: A Life Transformed by the Dearly Departing.

What do you think they are?

1. I would have preferred to live my life, not that of others.
2. I should have worked less.

3. I should have dealt with my feelings.
4. I should have stayed close to my friends.
5. I should have given myself the right to happiness.

When I read these responses, I thought it would make a great exponential routine to start my day by reminding me every day of the "essentials". So I reworded them in a positive way to read them every day:

1. Follow your dreams
2. Work less
3. Say what you think
4. Take care of your friends
5. Be happy

I suggest you do as I did and write down your ritual of success. The advantage of writing it down is that you can read it in a few seconds and check that you haven't forgotten anything. Once again, my own ritual of success lasts more than five minutes but that's normal, I'm the "Futurist Monk"! So, I invite you to choose the routines you like from this list, without exceeding the five-minute limit.

Here's my own ritual of success (roughly in the order I do my exponential routines):

- I go out to see the sun or natural light (or at least look out of a window, ideally an open one, if I can't get out easily).
- I meditate for at least twenty minutes (if you've never meditated, why not try just one minute of concentration, of *emptiness*?).
- I'm reading my vision, my dream: if there's only one exponential routine you need to remember, it's this one!
- I read my "essentials": "Follow your dreams," "Work less," "Say what you think," "Take care of your friends," and "Be happy."
- I do my yoga exercises and stretches (in my case, a few movements I learned on a trip to India, lasting about five minutes).

- I do my vocal exercises. One day in California, I met Roger Love, one of the world's best-known voice coaches (he trains Céline Dion, Eminem, Elton John...). I remember he asked me, "What's your most important tool in your life as a speaker?" As I hesitated between my frequent flyer cards, my remote control for my presentations and my computer, Roger told me the obvious: "It's your voice!" He then explained to me (and convinced me) that I was like a professional soccer player who never practiced and never warmed up before a match... Since that day, I've been practicing Roger's recommended vocal exercises (ten minutes) every morning. I also use them to warm up my voice before a conference.

- I send a "hug of love" to my loved ones: I started doing this routine because I felt I was missing the people I love, either because they lived far away or because I was away myself. It brings me a lot of peace. I asked them if they felt anything when I sent them my "love hugs". Their answer: not at all!

- I do my gratitude exercise: I look for three people, three events for which I feel gratitude. I'll come back to this routine in a few lines.

- I do my forgiveness exercise: I look for a person or an event that I forgive. This allows me to put the unpleasant event behind me and continue moving towards my dreams, my vision. Note that very often, I forgive myself...

The scars of life

Plastic surgeon Maxwell Maltz, whom we'll talk about in the paragraph on reprogramming the brain, tells of a patient who once asked him, "If scar tissue formation is a natural and automatic thing, why doesn't scar tissue form when a plastic surgeon makes an incision?" The answer is that if you cut your face and it heals naturally, scar tissue will form, because there's some tension in the wound and just below the wound that pulls the skin surface back creates a space that's filled with scar tissue. When a plastic surgeon operates, he or she not only tightens the skin with sutures, but also cuts away a small amount of flesh beneath the skin so that there is no tension. The incision heals smoothly, evenly and without distorting surface scarring.

> Maxwell Maltz explains that the same thing happens in the case of an emotional wound. If there is no tension present, no disfiguring emotional scar remains. Have you ever noticed how easy it is to "hurt" or "offend" yourself when you're suffering from tension caused by frustration, fear, anger or depression? Forgiveness is a scalpel that removes emotional scars. Forgiveness, when real, authentic and complete, is the scalpel that can remove the pus from old emotional wounds, healing them and eliminating the scar tissue. Forgiveness cuts away, eradicates, cancels out, makes the trauma we felt as if it never existed.

- I ask myself: what did I learn today (or yesterday)? This allows you to update and become aware of your progress or potential for evolution. For example: "I'm going to take ten minutes longer to get to this appointment", or "This relationship brings me more stress than pleasure, so I'm going to see less of her/him." It's a bit like the "lessons" in our annual review explained in the second chapter of this book for establishing our vision, our dreams, but in an express version.

- I read a book for fifteen minutes.

- I read my "big initiatives of the week": what I'd like to do this week as a priority. This allows me to choose a priority task for today.

- I mark this priority task, my *"One thing of the day"*, in my task manager.

- I don't check my e-mail before 11 a.m. I check my e-mail no more than three times a day (I'll come back to this point, which is the one that generally provokes the most... violent reactions!)

- I always check the news after 1 p.m. and I check it once a day at most. Starting your day by reading about all the misery in the world seems to me to be the perfect example of... negative self-amplification! You start the day with bad news. As a result, you're consciously or unconsciously in despair, so you're in a worse mood, so you've got less energy, so you're less creative, so you're less efficient, and so on.

- I only turn on my phone after my morning routine.

- I don't check my e-mail after 9 p.m. The only screen I allow myself in the evening is my tablet to read a book.

- I ask myself, "What am I going to look forward to today?" It's a great way to start the day in a good mood!

- I do a few minutes of cardiac coherence: if, like me, you're prone to stress or in a particularly stressful period, cardiac coherence is a very simple way of managing stress and emotions. You start the day less stressed, and as a result you're more efficient and focused on your vision and dreams. Personally, I do three three-minute heart coherences every day. There's plenty of information and tools on cardiac coherence on the Web.

- I read my express ritual: this is the ritual I do... when I don't have time to do my ritual of success. I'll show you how to do yours below.

- I reflect on my "highs" and "lows": which moments of the day (or yesterday) allowed me to be myself the most, to feel joy or fulfillment? And conversely, what were the moments that turned off my energy, when I felt bad or sad? If I ask you to tell me about your last vacation, you'll probably remember and tell me about the best and worst experiences you've had. This is because your memory doesn't record the "average" moments, but only the peaks of joy, happiness and fulfillment, or the peaks of sadness, discomfort or fear. As a result, our personality is shaped day after day by these memories, and only these. So it's very useful to be aware of them. It allows us to consciously decide what to do with them, and to learn from them. This is what we have already used to build our vision in the second chapter of the book.

- End the working day with a stopping ritual: separate the rest of your life from your work, close your laptop, plug in the charger, spend two minutes tidying up your desk. Say, "Yay, the workday is over!"

And one last routine: breaking routines. When I started using my daily ritual of success, I had decided to regularly "break" my routines and not follow them at least once a week. Many studies show that breaking the routines in your life can stimulate new parts of our brain. Doing the opposite of what comes naturally can activate the other side of our brain. For example, write with your left hand (if you're right-handed), play table tennis with the opposite hand, use the computer mouse with your other hand - in short, make your brain uncomfortable to stimulate it!

Choose the routines that seem most suited to your current life, those that seem easiest to put in place and those that seem to have the greatest potential self-amplifying effect in your own life. The only important rule is: I'm not asking you to believe me, I'm inviting you to try, adapt and adopt... or not!

- Try it for a few weeks and carefully observe the effects and results on your life.

- Adapt each routine to your reality. For example, for me, while it's fairly easy to be regular and do my routines well in the morning, it's much harder in the evening. For you, if you have to take care of your children in the morning or leave early for work, it may be the opposite and easier in the evening than in the morning.

- Adopt or not: if you don't notice any changes after a few weeks, or if the routine starts to bore you, try another one!

E-mails...

Many books have been written on how to deal with e-mails. Given the importance of e-mails in most of our professional and personal lives (if you're over 40...), I encourage you to read at least one of these books. I'd just like to mention here the importance of e-mails in relation to your ritual of success.

A few years ago, when I wanted to give an example of an exponential routine, I would logically choose one that has changed my personal and professional life the most, thinking that it would be the most useful to my interlocutors: I don't check my e-mails before 11 in the morning. In return, I usually received at best stunned looks, at worst sometimes violent reactions: "But you don't realize what you're saying, if I don't check my e-mails, my boss will kill me...".

Please note that the time for reading e-mail (11 a.m. or noon for me) is not the same for everyone. For you, it may be 9 a.m. or 3 p.m. The important thing is to consciously choose to give yourself time to manage your own priorities before managing those of others.

I would sum up my advice as follows:

- if you work for a hotline and your job is to answer users' e-mails, then answer the e-mails! I may be waiting for your reply...
- if you don't work for a hotline, then your e-mails can surely wait for the five minutes you're about to devote to your ritual of success. Deal with your priorities (the exponential routines that will help you achieve your dreams, your vision) before letting other people's priorities impose themselves on you. Otherwise, you're already working for other people's dreams (which may not be compatible with your own...).

Of course, this advice also applies to social networks. Although I'd say that when it comes to social network, it's even better not to go there at all!

And when I don't even have five minutes: the express ritual

I regularly find that my morning is rushed and that it's difficult to do my ritual of success calmly and correctly: I have to catch a train, I'm preparing to give a talk, I have guests at home (although in which case I'll often hide away in my room to do my routines...) For all these cases, I've developed an express ritual that takes me less than a minute and that I can do in almost any context.

To prepare your express ritual, I suggest you set aside an hour or so and follow the steps below.

- Meditate for a few minutes or go for a walk in nature or by the water.
- Answer the question: what three words best describe you?
- Meditate again for a few minutes or go for a walk in nature, by the water.
- Answer the question: what three words define your ideal interactions with others?

- Meditate again for a few minutes or go for a walk in nature, by the water.
- Answer the question: what three words will define your success?

To answer each question, as for the realization of your vision in the second part of this book, don't look for an answer, just let what comes naturally emerge. And if nothing comes today, that's okay, you can try again another day.

Write down your answers somewhere. And there you have it: your express ritual. Now it will only take you a few seconds to visualize the nine words you found in the previous exercise. If you wish, you can repeat this exercise regularly, changing the words you visualize during your express ritual.

By way of example (and as always, you are of course free to copy me...):

- the three words that describe the best of myself: *love, peace and harmony*
- the three words that define my ideal interactions with others: *loving, inspiring, reliable*
- the three words that will define my success: *learning, visionary and evolutionary*

Seeing these words, even very quickly, is enough to align you for the day towards your vision, your dreams. It's almost like an "express strange attractor"... And in any case, it's sure to put you in a good mood! As usual, I'm not asking you to believe me, I'm inviting you to try, adapt (to your personality, your context) and adopt or not (if it works for you or not).

Your mindset pack

You now have everything you need to make your "mindset pack", not only to survive in increasingly chaotic times, but also to take advantage of the opportunities of these times, because you've realized that you've never had so much power to change your life and create emergences for yourself, your loved ones, your community and humanity. Take your mindset pack with you wherever you go. Unless, of course, you prefer to wait for the collapse with your axe deep in the forest!

Your "mindset pack" is :

- your vision, your dreams
- your ritual of success
- your express vision

You can stop there if you like. You've got the gist! I invite you to try it for a few weeks and observe the changes in your life. And if, in a few weeks' time, you like these changes and you also notice that you're more efficient, more focused and have managed to free up time in your day, then you can choose to go even further. So, I'm now going to share with you some exponential routines that take more time and that you can choose to incorporate later into your ritual of success if you have the time and inclination. We'll then look at exponential routines that can be used by a group of people like a family or a team.

How to reprogram your brain to overcome your limiting beliefs

In the 1950s, plastic surgeon Maxwell Maltz was astonished, even dismayed, to find that his work didn't always have the expected psychological effect on his patients. He would receive patients who explained that they had an "ugly" nose that prevented them from leading a normal life. In some cases, these patients' noses looked perfectly normal, even very pretty, but he couldn't convince his patients. Nothing helped: their lives were hell because of their noses. When, at the end of his rope, he agreed to operate on these patients in the hope that it would still have a positive impact on their lives (by making a very minor modification to their noses), he found that their lives changed completely: "Thank you, Doctor, thanks to you my life has changed, I'm beautiful, other people's opinions have changed, and I'm much more successful at what I do." For Maxwell Maltz, this made no sense: he had done practically nothing, and the patient's life had changed completely! Conversely, he sometimes operated on people with very serious real aesthetic handicaps, and despite the success of the operation and the radical change in appearance, these patients continued, in their view, to live miserable lives. No matter how many people around them sincerely said to them: "I can't believe how much you've changed, you've become really beautiful", they would reply:

"No, don't lie to me, the operation failed, my nose is the same as before, I'm still just as ugly and that still handicaps me just as much in life." For Maxwell Maltz, it still didn't make sense: he'd made a huge cosmetic change and his patient's life hadn't changed at all! Maxwell Maltz came to the conclusion that there was no link between the real image of the people he had operated on and the image they had of themselves. And that their happiness, their way of life, was linked to their self-image, and not at all to reality! And that in many cases, to help his patients be happier, it would surely be more effective to help them change their self-image than to break out the scalpel. He wrote a book about it, *Psycho-cybernetics*, which is still today, over sixty years later, a personal development "bible".

What Maxwell Maltz teaches us is that you can accelerate the realization of your dreams by becoming precisely the person capable of realizing those dreams! All you have to do is change your self-image today. Put another way, if you become your "You 2.0", what seems difficult or impossible to achieve today will seem very easy tomorrow (or say, in a few weeks' time), or at the very least, very realistic. By consciously changing small daily habits, you're not changing small things, you're reprogramming the DNA of your behavior. You may not be able to realize your dream with your current habits, so change them! Your new, improved self will easily achieve them. In this way, you can reprogram your brain to react the way YOU want it to, not the way past habits, or the old self-image, automatically make it react.

To do this, you have two incredible tools at your disposal:

- *constructive imagination verses* to correct and heal the past
- *General Operating Principles* to move forward

Let's start with constructive imagination verses. These will enable you to let go of what we call your "limiting beliefs", the negative aspects of your self-image. Part of our brain is programmed... to fail! Our parents, family and school have imposed limiting beliefs on us that we carry as a burden for the rest of our lives:

- I'll never make it
- I'm not good at this or that
- I don't know how to put myself forward

- Don't talk to strangers
- I can never see my projects through to the end
- etc.

You can learn to identify these limiting beliefs and, more importantly, get rid of them!

The first step is to identify your own limiting beliefs. You can get help: our loved ones usually identify them even more easily than we do...

Then write the corresponding constructive imagination verses with the following formula:

FORMULA = I [final state of when I have what I want]. I feel [EMOTIONS AND FEELINGS I FEEL IN MY BODY WHEN I HAVE WHAT I WANT].

As an example, here are some of my own limiting beliefs and several constructive imagination verses I've written to get rid of them:

- Limiting belief: at 54, I've never done bodybuilding, it's not for me. I've tried a gym, but it's not for me and I'll never enjoy it.
- Constructive imagination verse: *"I like to push myself physically. I feel pleasure in the effort and joy in seeing my body progress."*
- As a result, I'm entering my sixth year of weight training, three times a week... and I can't believe I'm actually enjoying it!

- Limiting belief: I'm sometimes so paralyzed by a task that I give up and put it off until tomorrow.
- Constructive imagination verse: *"I love to act. I feel brave and euphoric when I act and I create enormous momentum and prosperity when I act."*
- As a result, I was able to write this book!

- Limiting belief: what I do is useless and of no interest to anyone.
- Constructive imagination verse: *"I know how to make my subject evolve to contribute to human evolution by touching the "right" people (the*

butterfly effect: one person can change the world, it's not a question of quantity...). And I feel joy in observing change in as many people as possible."

- As a result, I'm embarrassed to say that my conferences have been a success for years.

- Limiting belief: what I'm doing isn't very good and has certainly been said by others before me. Who am I to believe that I can change the world? (This is a classic and is called "impostor syndrome").

- Constructive imagination verse: "*I'm confident that I'm capable of improving my content in both form and content, and of making it evolve. I feel pleasure in offering my vision and tools to my audiences.*"

- Result: It helps me enormously when I need to talk to someone about my keynotes or my work. It gives me confidence.

- Limiting belief: I'm never lucky, it never works out.

- Constructive imagination verse: "*I have a posture that attracts serendipity and miracles. I attract success and abundance. Success and good things come to me naturally. Abundance and prosperity come to me from all directions. I feel euphoric. I look forward to waking up every day knowing that success is guaranteed for me.*"

- Result: it gives me energy and, faith, and ultimately (I believe) a lot of luck in life.

- Limiting belief: I don't like to "sell myself" and put myself forward to "sell" my keynotes to my interlocutors (and sometimes potential clients).

- Constructive imagination verse: "*I'm proud to transmit my message and my tools. I know my message is important, and I feel the joy of making an impact on my audiences.*"

- As a result, I now enjoy talking about my ideas and why they are important to my potential contacts and customers.

- Limiting belief: I easily brood and have obsessive negative thoughts.
- Constructive imagination verse: "*Every day, I take my happy pill. My actions and decisions are free of annoyance and irritation. I feel totally detached and protected from negative emotions and anger.*"
- Result: I quickly identify my negative thoughts and they easily disappear.

- Limiting belief: I have too much resistance to change, I'm tired of always having to change my work.
- Constructive imagination verse: "*My exchanges with my mentors, peers and friends help me evolve and adapt my discourse and actions to reach as many people as possible. I get a thrill out of evolving.*"
- As a result, I enjoy coming up with new ideas and developing my keynotes, seminars and thinking in general.

If some of my constructive imagination verses seem a little ridiculous, that's normal! They're tailor-made for my own brain... And of course my reality was very different when I originally wrote them and today, that's the point!

Now it's your turn!

- Identify three limiting beliefs
- Write the three corresponding lines of constructive imagination verse
- Visualize them every day for three weeks. When you do this visualization exercise, feel the emotion of the final state with intensity

And remember: once again, I'm not asking you to believe me, I'm inviting you to try it (three weeks), adapt (to your context and by evolving your constructive imagination verses over time) and adopt or not (if it doesn't work, choose another constructive imagination verse).

Create your new Personal Operating System

"Everything begins with a choice."
Morpheus

As we mentioned in the previous paragraph, you can make your dreams come true by becoming your "You 2.0" (or 3.0, 4.0, etc.). And what seems difficult or impossible today will seem easy tomorrow (or in a few weeks' time) because you'll no longer be the same person. You'll have become the person you want to be. A bit like a computer, we operate with our own *Operating System*, our OS. This "OS" is the result of years of conditioning, successes, failures, pleasures and frustrations. The accumulation of these events conditions us, mostly unconsciously, and makes us react in ways we don't always want to. However, it is possible to decide how we want to react and not let the conditioning of the past "freewheel" for us.

We've just seen how we can free ourselves from the conditioning resulting from our limiting beliefs with *constructive imagination verses*. Now let's see how you can reprogram your brain to react the way *you* want it to according to the events you're about to encounter. Here, it's no longer a question of overcoming our limiting beliefs, but of building our way of reacting to future life events according to your own wishes. The *General Operating Principles* help you to progress towards becoming the person you want to be. The person for whom it will then be easy to achieve your dreams.

Great athletes know that the brain can't tell the difference between what's real and what's imagined. So do as they do and learn how to make your brain react the way you want it to. Set up your new *Operating System*. Become your "You 2.0"! All you have to do is write down how you'd like to react in a given situation... and visualize it every day. Then simply let your brain do the work. There's nothing else to do!

> **Magic Johnson's virtual training**
>
> A journalist once asked champion basketball player Earvin Johnson Jr. aka "Magic Johnson" why he was so successful, especially at free-throw shooting. Magic Johnson replied that he had practiced tens of

thousands of times. The journalist, by simple mental calculation, came to the conclusion that the sportsman must be exaggerating, as it would have taken him several lifetimes to shoot that many free throws in training. The journalist then dared to express his doubts to Magic Johnson, who replied that he had of course included all the free throws he made in his imagination when he went to bed, when he got up, when he ate, when he jogged, when he travelled, and so on.

A few years ago, I remember listening to an interview with Jocko Willink, a former Navy Seal known for his books on the borderline between personal development and management. He explained how he had had to change his mindset in the face of the difficult circumstances he encountered in combat situations (particularly in Iraq). When faced with an unpleasant or dramatic situation (reinforcements not arriving on time, new weapons not delivered, insufficient time to prepare, etc.), he would force himself to think: "*It's good!*" You'll find this "*It's good!*" in my own list of *General Operating Principles* below. I adopted it several years ago, and I promise you that every time I encounter a difficult situation, my brain automatically reflexively says: "Bruno, *it's good!* Look for the hidden opportunities in this situation." And I can assure you that this completely changes my state of mind and my ability to deal with the difficult situation. It's incredibly effective. And as always, I'm not asking you to believe me, I'm inviting you to give it a try.

Here's a list of examples of *General Operating Principles, my "personal principles"* that I use or have used. After a while - usually a few weeks - they become so automatic that I no longer need to read them regularly. It just works!

Examples:

- *I live as if I'm going to live a very long time and as if I'm going to die tomorrow.* I used to visualize, "I live as if I'm going to live forever and as if I'm going to die tomorrow." And then I realized that I'm not a fan of the idea of living forever, I prefer the idea of one day leaving the place to new generations. Even if I'm not in too much of a hurry...

- *I think "and", not "or".* I observed that, on many occasions, it was either possible to do both, or it gave me new ideas.

- *I'm super demanding AND super indulgent with myself and others.*

- *I connect my thoughts to "only positive": every day, I let go of negative thoughts.* Whenever I have a negative thought, this phrase comes to mind... and helps me get rid of the negative thought.

- *I am wholeheartedly, fully present in every conversation I have with my interlocutors.* As soon as I start to think about something else when someone is talking to me, I refocus on what they're saying. And if I can't, or I'm really not interested, I politely excuse myself and walk away.

- *I only try to influence people when it can have a practical impact.* I give up trying to convince someone if it doesn't have a practical impact on their life, mine or the world. I avoid sterile arguments on general subjects.

- *My life and my choices are guided by what is beautiful, good and true.*

- *I don't say "yes but". I'm saying "yes and".* I will develop this point further in collective exponential routines.

- *I don't listen to my fears when I have to make a decision. I even go along with the fears.* This allows me to listen less to my fears, not to let them block me, and thus to make faster progress towards my dreams.

- *When I have to make a decision, I ask myself what I'd like to have chosen ten years from now.* This is one of the principles I've retained from reading the book (which I recommend) *Decisive* by Chip Heath and Dan Heath.

- *I focus on my circle of influence. I don't worry about the things I don't influence.* This is one of The *Seven Habits of Effective People*. It's a personal development book written by Stephen Covey and sold over 15 million copies worldwide (Covey Stephen, The 7 Habits Of Highly Effective People, Simon & Schuster, 2020)

- *Seek first to understand, only then to be understood.* It's another of Stephen Covey's *Seven Habits of Effective People*.

- *I ignore verbal aggression. They slide over me without getting to me. I take three breaths and move on.* When someone insults you, you have the choice of letting it get to you, or treating it as part of the ambient noise... That's what the personal principle helps you to do automatically.

- *Every day I'm super intense and uncompromising in my actions and intentions to achieve my goals and I know that at the same time I'm detached from the outcome.* I feel confident and relieved knowing that if I don't reach my goal today, it's "ok".

- *I go into "Terminator" mode when one of my projects is 85% complete.* Once I'm 85% done with a project, I start obsessively focusing on finishing it. I know my mind will play all sorts of tricks to distract and seduce me with a new project. I don't give in and finish the project at 100%.

- *I stop reading a book or an article when it doesn't bring me enough, bores me or depresses me.*

- *No guilt, always conscience.*

- *When I have to make a decision a year from now, I ask myself what I would do if it were this week.* That way, I don't get too excited about something I might not want to do in a year's time.

- *"It's good".* As explained above, no matter how well prepared you are for a crisis, something will happen that you haven't planned for. Accept it and improve your system for next time.

- *I prioritize and execute.* This principle was also suggested to me by Jocko Willink mentioned earlier. He recounts a situation in which he found himself in great danger with his Navy Seal patrol in Iraq, isolated from reinforcements, without enough ammunition and with a wounded man. What should he do? The list of important things he has to deal with is too big for a human brain. So, he chooses three priority tasks and carries them out without question. When I feel overwhelmed by events, when I have too many tasks to complete, my brain immediately reminds me automatically (that's what principles are for): "Bruno, prioritize and execute!"

- *I use Socrates' three filters.*

The Socrates' test

In ancient Greece, Socrates was reputed to hold knowledge in high esteem.

One day an acquaintance met the great philosopher and said,

"Do you know what I just heard about your friend?"

"Hold on a minute," Socrates replied.

"Before telling me anything, I'd like you to pass a little test. It's called the Triple Filter Test."

"Triple filter?"

"That's right," Socrates continued.

"Before you talk to me about my friend, it might be a good idea to take a moment and filter what you're going to say. That's why I call it the triple filter test.

The first filter is Truth.

Have you made absolutely sure that what you are about to tell me is true?"

"No," the man said, "actually I just heard about it and..."

"All right," said Socrates.

"So you don't really know if it's true or not.

Now let's try the second filter, the filter of goodness.

Is what you are about to tell me about my friend something good?"

"No, on the contrary..."

"So," Socrates continued, "you want to tell me something bad about him, but you're not certain it's true.

You may still pass the test though, because there's one filter left: the filter of usefulness.

Is what you want to tell me about my friend going to be useful to me?"

"No, not really."

"Well," concluded Socrates, "if what you want to tell me is neither true nor good nor even useful, why tell it to me at all?"

With that, he left, leaving him stunned by his questions.

- *When faced with difficult, unpleasant or dramatic circumstances, I accept it and serenely take action.* This effectively complements the previous "*It's good*" and enables me to accept life's sometimes difficult circumstances with greater serenity, to stop complaining unnecessarily and to take action to improve the situation.
- *I practice my pitches on every occasion. I always end with: "How can I help you?"* This helps me develop the reflex of offering people the opportunity to help me (see next paragraph on pitches).
- *Shut up and do something. Don't just sit there hesitating. Just do something. The answer will follow.* This is a good way to get out of stuck or procrastinating situations in your projects.
- *I know I am what I do. If I don't do it now, I never will. Each action is not an isolated event, but the setting up of a new neural pathway for the creation of a habit.* As Charles Duhigg explained so well in *The Power of Habits* and more recently James Clear in his book *Atomic Habits*, the brain constantly adapts by creating new neural pathways. It is therefore possible to change or create a new habit. The choice of whether or not to eat that cake, whether or not to exercise, is not an isolated event, but the beginning of the creation of a habit...
- *I know that vulnerability and authenticity are the path to true connections and quality relationships.* I seek to show vulnerability and authenticity, especially when the situation and social circumstances encourage me to do the opposite.
- *I follow the Toltec Agreements (*by Miguel Ángel Ruiz).

> **The Toltec Agreements**
>
> Born to a curandera mother and a Toltec shaman father, Miguel Ángel Ruiz studied medicine to become a surgeon. His life was turned upside down by a near-death experience that inspired him to seek answers to life's questions in the Toltec tradition. His book, published in 1997, has sold over 4 million copies. The five agreements in question can be summed up as follows:
>
> "*Let your word be impeccable.*" Speak with integrity, say only what you really mean. Use the power of speech for truth and love. Speech is a tool that can destroy. Be aware of its power and master it. Don't lie or slander.

> "*Whatever happens, don't make it personal.*" You are not the cause of other people's actions. What others say and do is only a projection of their own reality, dreams, fears, anger and fantasies. When you're immune to this, you're no longer a victim of needless suffering.
>
> "*Don't make assumptions.*" Don't start making assumptions about negative probabilities, only to end up believing them, as if they were certainties. Have the courage to ask questions and express your true desires. Communicate clearly with others to avoid sadness, misunderstandings and drama.
>
> "*Always do your best.*" There is no obligation to succeed; there is only an obligation to do your best. Your "best" changes from moment to moment. Whatever the circumstances, simply do your best and you'll avoid judging yourself, feeling guilty and having regrets. Attempt, undertake, try to make the best use of your personal abilities. Be indulgent with yourself. Accept that you're not perfect or always victorious.
>
> "*Be skeptical but learn to listen.*" Don't believe yourself or anyone else. Use the power of doubt to question everything you hear: is it really the truth? Listen to the intention behind the words and you'll understand the real message.

- *I treat every encounter as a "curiosity meeting"*. I try to go beyond small talk and treat every encounter as an opportunity to find out more about the person I'm talking to. I'm always amazed at the number of times a lunch or dinner that started out as boring with uninteresting people has turned, thanks to a few questions, into an incredible and profound encounter with people full of hidden resources. Here are my favorite questions (I don't hesitate to get out my notes to ask them when I can't remember). Choose one or two and give them a try:

    – What do you spend most of your time on?

    – What's a typical day like for you?

    – What turns you on at the moment?

    – What are you looking forward to in the coming weeks?

    – What's the most exciting thing you've done recently?

    – What choices have you made in your life that have made you who you are today?

- What was your first success?
- Why did you decide to do what you do today?
- What brought you to live where you do?
- If today was your last day on Earth and you had to leave a manual, a three-sentence instruction manual for your daughter or son, for your family, what would you write in it?
- How can I help you?
- What are the main challenges in your life?
- What was your biggest surprise?
- At your level, what's your biggest problem?
- What are you most proud of?

- *Every night, I choose to wake up tomorrow feeling energized and excited.* This principle is one of my favorites, so magical does it seem in its effectiveness. The simple fact of programming your brain before going to sleep means that you'll wake up in better shape to tackle the day. Another example of self-amplification. Give it a try!

- *I believe in focus.* Every day, I ask myself what's the ONE THING I can do so that by doing it, everything else is easier or unnecessary? It's the "*One Thing*" I mentioned earlier in my ritual of success.

- *I delay my judgment.* Often I think I've understood before the person has even finished speaking. Or I judge too quickly: "That's good", "That's bad", "I agree", "I disagree". I want to avoid this and take the time to give my interlocutor or events the chance to express themselves fully.

> **The mother, the little girl and the apple**
>
> A little girl hold an apple in both hands. Her mother enters the room. With a big smile on her face, the mother says gently: "My darling, would you please give Mummy one of your two apples?" The girl looks at her mother for a few seconds, then suddenly takes a bite of the first apple and swallows it quickly. Mom's smile freezes on her face. No sooner has the daughter finished than she rushes off to take

> a bite of the second apple. At this point, the mother finds it increasingly difficult to hide her disappointment. Then the little girl holds out one of the two apples to her mom, saying, "Here, Mom, this one's the best."
>
> Moral of the story: no matter who you are, how experienced you are or how well-informed you think you are, always delay judgment. Give others time and opportunity to explain themselves. What you see is not necessarily what you think. Try not to jump to conclusions!!!

And to finish this list of suggested personal principles, here are those used by Maxwell Maltz himself, the plastic surgeon I told you about at the beginning of this chapter:

- "I'm as happy as can be"
- "I act more friendly towards others"
- "I am less critical and more tolerant of others, their faults, failures and mistakes"
- "I act as if my successes are inevitable
- "I don't let myself be influenced by pessimistic or negative thoughts"
- "I smile at least three times a day"
- "Whatever happens, I react calmly and intelligently"
- "I completely ignore all the pessimistic and negative things that I can't do anything about or change."

Give it a try !

- Choose a few *Personnal Operating Principles* from the list above, or create your own.
- Remember, be modest at first, don't exceed five minutes of routines per day.
- Visualize them every day for three or four weeks.

And remember: as always, I'm not asking you to believe me, I'm inviting you to try it (three weeks), adapt it (to your context) and adopt it or not (if it doesn't work for you, then choose another *Personal Operating Principles*).

> **Brainwashing?**
>
> One day, as I was discussing with a young friend the importance of routines and daily visualization, he replied, "But that's real brainwashing, your stuff!" Before answering, I asked him to check his "screen time" on his phone. Results: an average of three hours a day on TikTok, two hours a day on YouTube and I didn't keep track of his time on Instagram and Snapchat... So my answer is: "If you don't brainwash yourself with what you want to become as a person, then you're letting other people brainwash you and you're going to become what they want you to become..."

A special case: information processing

I'd like to share with you all the exponential routines and personal principles I use in the field of information processing, because I think they're so important in our world of infobesity that they deserve our attention.

After my talks, participants are often given the opportunity to ask questions. There are three types of question:

- questions asked "in public" when the floor is given to those who request it, often with a microphone that rotates around the room
- the questions I'm asked "in private" when the conference is over and most of the participants have left
- the questions I'm asked during the cocktail party that sometimes follows the conference

By far the most frequently asked question in the second category is: "I have children, what would you advise me to do for them in this rapidly changing world?" It's a question that particularly resonates with me, because it's what triggered my choice twenty years ago to leave my well-paid job and seek to understand the incredible transition we humans are undergoing.

And to this question, which I often have to answer in just a few minutes, my two main answers are:

- teach them to learn, teach them to unlearn and teach them to relearn. Of course, this also applies to us older children: learn to learn, learn to unlearn and learn to relearn
- teach your children how to process increasingly abundant information, how to find it, qualify it and interpret it. And that also goes for older children too...

It's an increasingly important issue for all of us. In the past, censorship worked by blocking the flow of information. In the 21ST century, censorship works by inundating people with irrelevant information. In ancient times, having power meant having access to data. Today, having power means knowing what to ignore. Put another way, with so much going on in our chaotic world, what should we focus on? I'd like to share with you how I'm responding to this challenge myself: learning how to process increasingly abundant information in an efficient and relevant way.

HOW DO YOU FIND, QUALIFY AND INTERPRET INFORMATION?

I think this question is particularly important when you're going through a period of crisis or chaos, either personally or collectively. So I'm going to share it with you:

- the basic principles I use in a crisis to process information and decide
- how I process information in general
- some thoughts on information and the media.

At the time of the terrorist attack in Paris on November 13, 2015 (also know as the Bataclan attack), I was a long way from the events in my resilient home in the South of France. I remember that this evening several supposedly reliable news sources (the information had been broadcast on a major national radio station and picked up by most of the other media) were reporting "Kalashnikov shots" in the Halles district of Paris, where I have a small apartment and where I regularly live. This information turned out to be false, as no shots were fired in the area. I wondered what I should have done if I'd been in Paris that evening. Barricade myself in? Run away as fast as I could? A few weeks later, I had lunch with Patrick Lagadec, who I consider one of the world's leading experts in crisis management. I had met Patrick when my first book was published over thirty years ago. We spent the day together promoting our respective books from the same publisher at an event in Deauville, Normandy. I asked him for his advice in such a situation.

Here's his answer:

- turn off all sources of information: Internet, radio, television
- prepare a list of questions to which you would like answers (less than 10 questions) in order to make your decision (in this case, for example, should you stay barricaded at home or leave as quickly as possible to find shelter elsewhere?)
- reopen your information channels and consult a limited number of media you can access for an equally limited time (ten-thirty minutes max depending on circumstances) to try to get as many answers as possible to these questions and only these questions
- when you've answered more than half your questions to the best of your ability (not perfectly), turn off all the information channels again
- make the best decision based on this limited and insufficient information
- execute the decision
- be ready to abandon your initial patterns, your habitual reflexes, your preparations for previous crises if you feel that in the current situation "the rules no longer apply"

This was obviously an extreme and dramatic example. But I find it very useful and inspiring in an increasingly chaotic world. I've adapted them for the less dramatic but sometimes destabilizing events of everyday life:

- *I go hunting for information. Information doesn't come to me.* I choose the information channels I want to consult, not social networks or my "friends". You can find out more about my information sources and how I choose them here: https://brunomarion.com/information

- *I'm ready to abandon my maps, my reference points and my usual ways of acting in a second if I feel they no longer apply.* When the situation goes beyond the usual or pre-prepared cases, I don't hesitate to abandon my habits and reflexes, and I show freedom and creativity

This is one of the personal principles I visualize every day. I actually used Patrick Lagadec's method several times during the Covid-19 crisis. For example, to answer the following questions:

- Do I have to join my family now (I was travelling when it all started)? And if not, when should I return?

- Do I have to wear a mask for my return trip (at the time, very few people wore masks where I was)?

- Should I take a preventive treatment?

- Should I advise my parents to stay at home (this was long before the official lockdown)?

- Do I go food shopping at the start of the lockdown or do I stay at home as much as possible?

Which leads me to share with you how I deal with information more generally. It can be summed up like this: I protect myself from infobesity. I limit my exposure to the media to twenty minutes a day. Only once a day, always after mid-day. And never when I wake up (when my critical faculties are still a little asleep...). I particularly apply this rule in times of crisis, when I'm most tempted to look at a lot of information... and when, on the contrary, I want to keep as much perspective as possible which would not be possible with a continuous flow of information (usually repeated in a loop). I'm absolutely fascinated and horrified by the people who listen to radios or watch 24-hour news channels. Not only does it fail to respect the previous principle: "I go hunt for information, it's not the information that comes to me", but it seems to me to be a form of deliberate brainwashing (dumbing down?) I also avoid social networks, which also go against the principle: "I go hunt for information. It's not the information that comes to me". Indeed, in the case of social networks, it's their algorithm that chooses for me what information I can read. And I don't want to let Facebook's or X/Twitter's algorithm decide for me what I should or shouldn't know.

I go to the source

I don't form a definitive opinion after reading three Facebook articles (or even just one, as seems to be the case more and more). For me, going to the source means, for example, if an article talks about a study, I try to find and read that study. You don't have to do this for every article you read, but it's a good idea to do it when you feel that what you're reading is making you form an opinion on a subject.

I remember the debate (should I say religious war?) between French Professor Didier Raoult's supporters on the treatment of Covid and his opponents. In this case, to try to make up my mind, I read the 62-page report of the Senate Commission on the subject and watched two one-hour interviews with Didier Raoult. And I did the same with the opposing opinions. And I concluded... that I couldn't conclude! That if all these experts, some of whom seem to me to be sincere and knowledgeable about their subject, can't agree, well, the best solution for me, far from being an expert on these subjects, was to be patient, humble and wait for new information. So, when I was asked my opinion on the subject, I would reply: "I don't know...".

Assessing the source

Going to the source also means checking and evaluating its quality and credibility. What other articles has the author written? Nowadays, it's often easy to find out what an author has written in the past, before the article I'm reading was published. So I often find other articles the author has written on subjects I may know more about, or which are old enough for me to assess their accuracy. If in a previous article, the author explains that the Earth is flat (sorry, we've known the Earth is round for a few hundred years) or that it's the end of the world in 2000 or 2012 (I wrote this book afterwards so *a priori* everything's fine), I don't take his point of view into account in his new article... And any mail, even from close friends, that starts with: "Watch this video before it's deleted", "I have a doctor friend who told me that...", or "What the media don't tell you" automatically go into trash...

I read books

I've noticed an increasing temptation among myself and those around me (especially younger people) to watch videos rather than read books or long articles (longer than 140 or 280 characters for example...).

YouTube rarely seems to me to be a valid source for going into depth in a field. There are a lot of YouTube channels that seem to me to be really well done, with serious youtubers who allow you to discover a subject. But there are also many that just skim the surface of their subject and whose sole aim is to get the most views and sell the most advertising. And then, without paying attention, it's very quickly the YouTube algorithm that chooses the next video for you. Which, once again, is not compatible with the previous principle: "I'm going to get the information. It's not the information that comes to me." To really learn and not just skim over a subject, to develop your critical faculties (for example, pausing to think), there's an incredible tool: a book!

I'm often asked how I manage to read around 100 books a year. It's very simple: I read for at least fifteen minutes every morning. It's part of my morning routine and therefore comes before the rest of the day. And I don't watch TV, listen to the radio and rarely go on social networks. You don't have to read as much as a futuristic monk. But you can experiment: try to read a dozen books a year, if you haven't already, and see what it's done for you in a year's time.

And no, this paragraph was not suggested to me by my publisher!

THE TYRANNY OF COMMUNICATION

Many years ago, I was struck by a book by Ignacio Ramonet, a French journalist. One of the ideas I retained was that quality information necessarily has a cost:

- either in terms of time: information is not easy to find, it takes time to research

- or in terms of resources: other people do the research for you, as in the case of a subscription to quality media or the purchase of a book

In other words, there's no such thing as free, easy, quality information (oops, sorry...). Another point I remember: all the media follow each other. When one says something, the others will say more or less the same thing to "stay in the race". And last but not least, advertising-driven media make you read what you want to read, so that you keep buying (or clicking). So they won't try to change your point of view. The presenters and journalists on many 24-hour news channels know their audience minute by minute. So they know precisely whether you liked what they just sad, or whether you skipped it! So they don't risk pushing you to change your mind...

How others can help you realize your dreams

You're not alone in the adventure! Other people, your friends, your colleagues, your family, your entourage, are just waiting to help you achieve your dreams... if you know how to call on them. And to get help, you first must help others to help you. And that starts with doing your homework! There are three tools you can use to give others the chance to help you if they want to:

- the mapping workshop
- your communication action plan
- your pitches

MAPPING WORKSHOP

Take a sheet of paper and write down the names of all the people you interact with in your life (daily or just once every ten years...). Try to be as exhaustive as possible. The idea is to have as many names as possible on the sheet: friends, family, colleagues, former colleagues, neighbors, anything you can think of. And it doesn't matter if you forget people, you can fill in with new names another day. The format doesn't matter; however, many people like to use the mindmap format for this exercise.

You now have as exhaustive a list as possible of the people you interact with on a more or less regular basis. You can now use this list to draw up your communication action plan.

COMMUNICATION ACTION PLAN WORKSHOP

Take each name from the map you obtained in the previous step and indicate how, and how often, you'd like to communicate with that person.

For example:

- Aunt Lola: a phone call once a year
- my colleague Marc: a coffee together at least once a week
- my school friend Philippe: a call every month
- John is like a mentor to me: one call a week

What counts in this exercise and in the mapping workshop is not so much the result. It's about forcing ourselves to be aware of our different relationships and consciously deciding how much energy we want to devote to them. In the old past, human relationships were formed naturally with those closest to us, whether geographically, through family or affection. Today, in the age of Skype, Zoom, Facebook, Instagram and TikTok, it's important to be aware of our relational network and to give it the attention we want, voluntarily and not just unconsciously.

YOUR PITCHES

The legend of the elevator pitch is that you should be able to present your project to your boss or to an investor you meet by chance in an elevator, in less than one or two minutes. I imagine that this approach to pitching has become a little outdated, and that today your boss or potential investor would ask you to send him an e-mail...

I've always felt very uncomfortable with the supposed need to "pitch". It's too "commercial", it's too "American", it's not for me, and so on. Besides, my introverted side means that I feel maximum anxiety as soon as someone asks me: "And what do you do for a living?" So, pitching, not really for me! Then I met my friend Herman, who lives in California, is the author of a book on pitching and has helped many start-ups with their projects. When I told him about my reservations regarding pitches, he simply "turned my head" and changed my mind by telling me: "You're being arrogant and pretentious Bruno, refusing to prepare a few sentences to offer your interlocutors the possibility of helping you if they feel like it". Well indeed, seen from that angle, it does look different! Since then, I've been working on my pitches, which I'll share with you, and I no longer feel anxious when people ask me what I do for a living. So, you too can offer others the chance to help you by making it easier for them: learn how to present yourself, what you like to do in life, or the projects you're passionate about now.

No pitch is meant to explain everything; on the contrary, it's meant to start a conversation, arouse the curiosity of your interlocutor and invite them to ask you questions.

Below, by way of example, are the pitches I personally use:

- **The one-word pitch:** one or two words that describe what you want to share. Ideally, this should trigger a question from your interviewer.

My one-word pitch: *The futuristic monk*. The question "What's a futuristic monk?" usually comes quickly... and the conversation begins!

- **The question pitch:** a question that invites the other person to think... and start a conversation.

My question pitch: "Do you think our children, your children if you have any, will live in a better world than ours?"

- **The subject line pitch**: just like an e-mail, a few words that make you want to open and read it.

My subject line pitch: "Chaos isn't messy!"

- **The Twitter pitch:** 140 or 280 characters to describe what you want to talk about.

My Twitter pitch: "Thrive in uncertainty, be more resilient and benefit from crises with new tools based on chaos theories."

- **The Pixar pitch:** It's the magic formula behind the success of all Pixar cartoons (*Toy Sory, Nemo, Monsters & Co.*, etc.):

    – Once upon a time...

    – Every day...

    – And one day...

    – Because of that...

    – And because of that...

    – Until finally...

My Pixar pitch: "At 36, I was childless and had every reason to believe that I wouldn't have a biological child. Because of this I began to wonder what my legacy would be since I wasn't going to pass on my genes... until finally I decided to quit my job to seek to understand the incredible transition I was seeing happening in the world and find and share the tools to create emergences in our personal and collective lives."

So find out, test, develop and bring your pitches to life on every occasion! And above all, practice! My favorite training ground: when taxi drivers ask me what I do for a living.

The 3-2-1: the way to avoid being stuck in the past

"Where THAT was, there I shall become."
Sigmund Freud

We saw in the previous paragraph on *constructive imagination verses* how we can free ourselves from our limiting beliefs and speed up the achievement of our dreams. But it's not just limiting beliefs that slow us down. There are also what we might call our "personal shadow areas" (or "shadows" for short). For this very powerful exponential routine, I drew inspiration from the integral approach and the book *Integral Life Practice* by Ken Wilber, which I highly recommend that you read.

What's a shadow? The word "shadow" refers to the aspects of yourself that you have repressed, hidden (hence the term "shadow"), rejected and then projected onto others. This is also known as the "repressed unconscious". It's often our shadows that make us feel irritated or angry with someone. They can also create fears and blockages.

How do our shadows form?

1. We have a desire or an emotion. But we can't realize it or express it (our parents, social conventions or context prevent us from doing so).
2. We project this emotion onto someone else (you never do...).
3. And then we project it onto others in general, or onto a group of people (people always do...).

So, first, I have an emotion (1st person "I"), which I project onto another person (2nd person: "YOU") and generalize to everyone (3rd person: "THEM" or "THEY"). In other words:

1. 1st person: "I"
2. 2nd person: "YOU"
3. 3rd person: "THEY" or "THEM".

You can easily recognize your shadows in two ways:

- either someone or something makes you negatively hypersensitive, easily reactive, irritated, angry, hurt or upset. This can translate into a negative emotional tone or a bad mood that permeates your life
- or, on the contrary, a person or something makes you positively hypersensitive, easily infatuated, possessive, obsessed, overly attracted, or perhaps becomes an idealization that structures your motivations or moods

For example:

1. I'm angry and I repress my anger. I don't like being angry and my environment doesn't allow me to express it (1st person)
2. I can't stand "your" tantrums anymore, for example to a friend... or in his relationship (2nd person)
3. 'People' are getting angrier and angrier because of social networks, and that bothers me a lot. Or 'my husband' is angrier and angrier, and I can't stand it anymore" (3rd person).

The process we're going to use is called "3-2-1", because it will work in reverse to free you from the shadow you initially created. In other words:

1. 3rd person: "THEY" or " THEM "
2. 2nd person: "YOU"
3. 1st person: "I"

Let's take a closer look at some examples. First, decide what you want to work on. It's often easiest to start with someone you're having trouble with (e.g., a lover, friend, boss, family member). This person may irritate, bother, annoy or upset you. Or perhaps, conversely, you feel attracted to, or positively obsessed by, this person. In any case, choose someone with whom you have a strong emotional charge, whether positive or negative.

3RD PERSON - FACE YOUR SHADOW

Sit down on a chair opposite another empty chair. Now imagine the person or situation that bothers you, makes you angry or, on the contrary, positively obsesses you, sitting on that empty chair in front of you. Describe this person, the situation and the feelings you're experiencing in as much detail as possible, using 3rd person pronouns such as "he", "him", "she", "her", "they", "their", "that" or "his". The first few times you do this exercise, I advise you to write down whatever comes into your head. With a little practice, it won't be so important to write it down, and you'll be able to do the exercise mentally and without a chair!

2ND PERSON - TALK TO HIM/HER

Start an imaginary dialogue with this object or person by imagining it sitting on the empty chair in front of you. Use 2nd person pronouns such as "you" and "yours". Speak directly to the person or image as if they were actually sitting in the chair. Tell her what bothers you about her. Ask her questions such as "Why are you doing this to me?", "What do you want from me?", "What are you trying to show me?", "What do you have to teach me?" Then allow him/her to respond. Imagine what her response to these questions would be, and speak the imaginary answers aloud, writing them down in your journal. Let yourself be surprised by what comes out.

1ST PERSON - EMBODY IT

Now go and sit down on the chair in front of you and fully take the place and embody the person who sat there before you. Speaking in the 1st person, using pronouns like "I", "me" and "mine", be that person, image or feeling. See the world, including yourself (imagine looking at and talking to yourself in the chair you sat in moments ago, which is now empty). Embody the person who positively or negatively bothers or obsesses you. Allow yourself to discover not only your similarities, but how you really are one and the same. Embrace the qualities that upset or fascinate you. Declare that you yourself are that person with expressions like "I'm...", "I'm angry", "I'm jealous", "I'm radiant." This may sound false or awkward. Yet the traits you're adopting are the traits you've denied in yourself. They're the traits your psyche has worked so hard to keep in the shadows.

To complete the process, gently become aware of the disowned qualities within yourself. Don't just see the world from this perspective but feel this previously excluded feeling until it resonates as your own. Experience the part of you that is this very trait. Avoid staying in your head and making the process abstract or conceptual: just be it. Become aware of the hitherto disowned shadow reintegrating itself into your body, memory and emotions.

Taking the previous example:

- 3rd person - Face your shadow: "I have a big problem with my husband, who is always angry"
- 2nd person - Talk to him: "I can't take it anymore, it's become unbearable, I don't dare tell you that you're still angry"
- 1st person - Embody it: "I understand that I too have angers that I don't allow myself to express. It's okay to feel angry. I'm going to learn to express my disagreements, my frustrations and my suffering."

Or another example:

- 3rd person - Face your shadow: "I can't stand my boss who is incapable of making a decision"
- 2nd person - Talk to him: "Why don't you ever decide anything? It prevents us from working efficiently, and we're wasting an awful lot of time"
- 1st person - Embody it: "I'm afraid I won't be effective, and I understand that sometimes it's better to take my time when there's no urgency to better study all aspects of an issue before making my decision."

You'll know the process has worked because you'll feel lighter, more peaceful, and certainly more relaxed and at peace. You can perform the 3-2-1 process whenever you need to. Two particularly useful times are when you wake up in the morning and just before you go to bed at night. Once you know the 3-2-1, it only takes a minute to perform the process for anything that might be bothering you.

Morning: before getting out of bed, review your last dream and identify any emotionally charged person or object. Face this person or object with it in mind. Then talk to that person or object. Finally, be that person or object from their perspective. For the purposes of this exercise, you don't need to write anything down. You can go through the whole process in your mind.

Evening: one last thing before going to bed, choose a person who has disturbed or attracted you during the day. In your mind, face him or her, then be him or her (as described above).

Weekly Review

Weekly reviews are the "routine of routines". These reviews will help you gain clarity and focus on what you want to do in the week ahead. These reviews help you regain clarity in an increasingly chaotic world. My weekly review takes me less than thirty minutes (often less than twenty) and in such a short time not only does it bring me clarity, but above all peace. I know I haven't forgotten anything and that I'm focused on the important things. After I've done it, I feel a bit like when I've done a "closet tidy-up", or when the car's just been serviced and everything's fine, or when my suitcases are ready before I leave on a trip: a sort of relief, peace and a desire to act.

The purpose of the weekly review is not to make major strategic decisions but rather to "clean up the week":

1. Tidy up your digital spaces (the "closet storage" aspect)
2. Update the to-do list for this week or later
3. Decide on your priorities for the week

I do it on Mondays, but many people prefer to do it on Sundays to start the week on the right foot. Personally, I prefer to save my Sunday for family and friends. Once again, try it, adapt it to your context and adopt it or not (depending on whether it works for you or not).

My weekly review process:

1. I empty my mail inbox: I empty my inbox completely. Each mail is either turned into a "task" in my to-do list, filed under

"things to read later" (for example, the few newsletters I've selected), or put in the trash. It's easy enough for me, as my mailbox is almost always empty if I regularly follow this process! If you have hundreds or thousands of e-mails in your inbox, I suggest you put them all in an "Archive" folder with today's date (you can always deal with them later, I'm sure most of them have been waiting for some time already...) and start the week with an empty inbox. And that's it!

2. I review my calendar: I take a quick look at the last two weeks and the next two weeks in my calendar to see if there are any to-dos I've forgotten about, related to past or upcoming events

3. I sort out the "Downloads" folder on my computer: I file the various files (usually by archiving them) or put them in the trash

4. I empty the inbox of my note-taking application: I use the Evernote application, which serves as my "second brain", storing all the information I want to keep. The notes I've made during the week are in the Inbox, so I file them in their respective folders or archive them

5. I write down my priorities for the week

6. I sort and update my to-do list

7. I sort my physical inbox: I sort my paper mail, the bills in my wallet and so on

8. I reboot my computer: this is usually the only reboot of the week, the rest of the time I just put it on standby to save time when I use it again

9. I clean my computer, my phone, my tablet: I'm always amazed at how much good a simple wipe does to me!

10. I back up my computer on an external disk (I also have automatic online backups)

11. I review my finances: a quick overview of my accounts (with my bank's application on my phone)

12. I close all web browser tabs on my computer, tablet and phone

13. I back up my phone: I check that my iPhone's automatic backup is recent, otherwise I make a new one

14. Backing up my tablet: same for my phone, but this time with my iPad

15. I check and delete spam: I go through the mails in my spam box. I check that there aren't any e-mails in there that shouldn't be there and that I need to deal with. I then empty the spam box, permanently deleting all other spam

16. I empty my computer's "recycle garbage can"

As always, I invite you to :

- **Try it:** observe carefully how you feel after doing your weekly review: Peace of mind? Clarity?
- **Adapt to your context:** choose the tasks from the list above that make sense to you. Feel free to leave some out or add your own. Try not to add too much either: the weekly review should remain a quick and "light" exercise, ideally lasting less than thirty minutes.
- **To adopt or not:** in a few weeks, update the list of tasks in your weekly review, keeping only those that are really useful to you. Drop the others or do them only once a month.

Playing together: group routines

One day, I was invited to a meeting at a small company in Paris. During the meeting, I was quickly intrigued by the presence of a little pink piggy bank in the middle of the meeting room table. And even more intrigued by the behavior of the participants: regularly, they all fell silent and one of them stood up to put a euro in the little pig! As I'm sure you've gathered from reading this book, my passion lies in identifying, understanding and sharing patterns, hidden orders and operating modes. So, as you can imagine, all my senses were on alert! And I quickly identified the rule the group had set themselves (which I later verified with them): every time a participant uttered a "yes but", they had to put a euro in the little piggy bank, and at the end of the month everyone took advantage of the kitty to enjoy a good meal or a drink together. The rule was abandoned after a while, as the objective had been achieved: hardly anyone used "yes but" in meetings anymore!

The group had chosen this rule for a simple reason: when you say "yes but", your interlocutors consciously or unconsciously hear "no because". And let's face it, it's hard to talk to and even harder to agree with someone who's constantly telling you "no". I invite you to try replacing your "yes-but's" with "yes-and's". This doesn't prevent you from expressing disagreement, quite the contrary: for example, "Yes, I hear your point of view AND I disagree completely AND I'm going to express my point of view AND I'm sure we'll come to an agreement." Try it, and you'll see that the energy and results of the conversation or meeting are very different.

Another day, I was to meet the head of a start-up company and one of his colleagues. As soon as I arrived and was taking off my coat (it was winter), my contact arrived and said, "Keep your coat on, we're going to have the meeting walking in the neighborhood." I was a little doubtful at the idea of having a meeting while walking in the center a city in the middle of winter... A few minutes was enough for me to observe how we discussed differently and were more open and creative than if we'd been sitting indoors in the warmth. I've since tried "walking meetings" many times, and I'm always blown away by what it brings. Even more so when you're lucky enough to be able to do it in nature rather than in the center a city!

Replacing "yes-but" with "yes-and" or walking meetings are the perfect examples of exponential routines with more than one person! Indeed, just as you can trigger big changes in your life by transforming small things in your life with exponential routines, you can also achieve big changes and bring out new behaviors in a group of individuals. So, just as you can create your individual ritual of success, you can share new "rules of the game", as if you wanted to play a new board game or card game, with your family or colleagues. The only essential difference is that for your ritual of success, you must agree only with yourself, whereas to choose the exponential routines you're going to experiment with when there are several of you, you'll have to choose with your fellow players.

> **Is culture a good investment?**
>
> At an Airbnb fundraiser, Peter Thiel's investment fund invested $150 million. The Airbnb team invited Thiel to their office and took him to a conference room where they displayed various metrics on screen to show him how the company was doing. In the middle of the conversation, Airbnb CEO Brian Chesky asked Thiel what was the most important piece of advice he had for them? You might think it would be something about gross margins or network effects that you'd hear about in an MBA program. It wasn't. His response was, "Don't screw up your culture." It wasn't what you'd expect from someone who had just written a check for $150 million. When asked to elaborate, he said that one of the main reasons he invested in Airbnb was their culture.
>
> Culture is a difficult thing to value because it is mostly invisible or illegible. It doesn't appear on a balance sheet or exist in the physical world. As a result, many people tend to ignore or minimize it.

The best way to convince others to adopt new rules of the game, a new culture, is to share how your own ritual of success and exponential routines have positively changed your life with specific examples. And as with your own success routine, don't forget to invite others to **try it** (don't impose it on them, it won't work), to be flexible and **adapt** it to the culture of your group of friends, the habits of your family or the corporate culture in which you operate. And be persistent, not stubborn, by deciding together whether or not to adopt the new "rules of the game", depending on whether or not they produce positive results after a few weeks.

Here is a list of collective exponential routines that I have experimented with or whose success I have observed in groups of people, companies, or simply families:

- Hold a minute's silence (or more, depending on the culture of the group or company) before starting a meeting

- Do a "weather tour": ask everyone to express their current context in one minute. This helps to bridge the gap between what was going on before and the meeting itself. It also gives those who wish to do so the opportunity to express a problem ("I'm a bit worried and not very focused on this meeting, because when I left home this morning my son was a bit ill"). It also often triggers more empathy in the group even before the exchanges begin

- Start a family gathering or meal by expressing the gratitude you feel for one of the other participants
- Holding meetings while walking, as in the story of my meeting with an executive in the streets
- Stand-up rather than sit-down meetings: here too, meetings are almost always much smoother, richer and more creative than when participants sit in their chairs and comfortably camp out in their positions...
- In the same vein, I attended a meeting where everyone was sitting on balloons!
- Use a talking stick: only the person holding the talking stick (or any other funny accessory - I visited a company where the talking stick was a stuffed giraffe...) is allowed to speak. This allows everyone to listen to each other and not talk at the same time
- As in the previous story of the little pig, replace the "yes-but's" with "yes-and's". This is certainly one of the most self-amplifying collective routines, the one that gives the most results day after day
- Do regular "Life swaps": swap jobs or functions for a day or longer. It's a radical way to reduce conflict... and it can even work between family members!
- Set a maximum length for meetings in advance. I remember once seeing that at Google in Brussels, meetings were limited to thirty minutes! I don't know if this rule is still in place
- Ask all your visitors (to your company or your home) for their astonishment reports: what surprised them during their visit?
- Bring your pet to the office (every day, once a month, once a week or once a year, depending on your company's culture)
- Ban words like "love" and "hate". At the non-profit organization DoSomething.org, CEO Nancy Lublin has banned employees from using words like "love" and "hate", as

they too easily allow a visceral response without analysis. Employees aren't allowed to say they prefer one web page to another; they must explain their reasoning with statements like "This page is stronger because the title is more readable than the other options." This motivates people to come up with new ideas rather than simply rejecting existing ones

- Appoint a "devil's advocate", whose role is to question or attack decisions made by the group. It's not uncommon to have many, too many, volunteers for this role, which is why it's so important to choose just one...

> **The saints' prossecutor**
>
> From 1587 to 1983, a person was appointed in the Vatican to argue against the possible canonization of a person. This person had to find the faults that the candidate had committed, faults that would obviously make it impossible for him or her to become a saint. It was a process that prevented a person from being canonized by mistake. After John Paul II stopped this practice, 500 people were canonized during his reign, compared with 98 during the reign of all his predecessors in the 20TH century...

Choose one or two collective exponential routines and try to implement them with your fellow players. And don't forget: invite others to try it out and adapt it to the culture of your group of friends, the habits of your family or the corporate culture in which you operate. And decide together whether or not to adopt the new "rule of the game" depending on whether or not it produces positive results after a few weeks.

And if you consider that you are, or want to be, a leader in your organization, your team or simply your family or a group of friends, the role of the leader in a chaotic world is no longer to make all the decisions. His role is to create the right context, a context favorable to emergence. And that means, as we've seen, taking care to create and nurture:

- a dream, a utopia, that you repeat to everyone day after day. Define and share your strange attractor. And let me remind you, as we saw in the second chapter, that not everyone needs to have the same dream. Dreams just have to be compatible with those who "get on your boat" or decide to play with you

- a set of routines and rituals to benefit from the butterfly effect and/or create emergences. "At home, we do things this way, we play cards this way. It's our "culture".

A shared dream gives hope, and routines and rituals provide a sense of security and reinforce trust between group members. As usual, I'm not asking you to believe me, I'm inviting you to give it a try!

The guru who doesn't believe in gurus

Often, when I talk to company directors, I feel a sort of "disappointment" when they discover the tools I'm sharing with them. They seem too simple. I get the feeling that they're expecting THE miracle solution from the new management guru. Thirty years ago, a new management guru would regularly come along with a revolutionary new management method: Peter Drucker, Gary Hamel... And everyone would apply it. And it worked. Now I explain to them that I'm the guru who doesn't believe in gurus! Today's leader brings a vision, a shared dream, a strange attractor and a "culture": How we play cards together, what are the rules, rituals and routines in my company? I used to ask these managers: 'Why do you think young people spend more time on Facebook than working on their objectives in some companies, while in other companies or NGOs, where they are sometimes paid less, they work their asses off and don't count their hours?' The difference: they share the dream of the leader(s). And they feel comfortable in the specific culture of that particular company (and not necessarily that of another).

How to surround yourself with reliable people

To conclude both the collective aspects of exponential routines and this third part of the book, I'd like to share with you one last example of self-amplification, which is very important to me: reliability in relationships.

I remember a friend who refused to start a serious project with other people, whether it was a business project or simply going on vacation with friends, without first doing the "dinner test". He would propose a dinner with all concerned and observe:

- who offered to organize the dinner (choice of restaurant, times, etc.)

- who needed to ask three times about the day, time and place of dinner
- who was on time... or not
- who paid his share... or not

His idea was that if people were reliable for a simple dinner, they would probably be reliable for a more ambitious project or vacation together. And vice versa... If these people weren't reliable for something as simple as dinner, according to my friend, they wouldn't be any more reliable for a more ambitious project. My friend had indeed consciously and intentionally decided to surround himself with reliable people.

I'd like to show you that this is increasingly important today, and that my friend's dinner test is perhaps even more important. Because the more reliable you are, the more you'll be surrounded by people who are too. And vice versa. The phenomenon of self-amplification that we've discussed many times in this book also applies today more than ever to this aspect of our relationships with others, as in my friend's dinner test: reliability. In the old world, most people lived in a small community: a village, a small town or the neighborhood of a big city. Everything was known. If you weren't reliable, if you weren't trustworthy, people knew very quickly. So it was obvious that taking care of your image in your community was important. We were sensitive to reliability (we could also speak of trust) because the social context constantly reminded us of it. Our ancestors always consciously or unconsciously paid close attention to their reputations. Then, little by little, many people joined the anonymity of big cities... and then of the virtual world. Exchanges are increasingly taking place online, at a distance. And we got used to living in a kind of anonymity and a certain lack of responsibility. The consequences of our actions have become less and less important. If you insult someone on Facebook, or behave like a troll, who knows? Who cares? What are the consequences? In the old world, if you insulted everyone in a small village, you quickly paid the consequences, usually some form of exclusion. Not so much on Facebook or Twitter...

Paradoxically, thanks to or because of self-amplification phenomena, the importance of reliability, of our reputation, is coming back with a vengeance after a few decades of indifference. In fact, our digital reputation is being built up bit by bit... Our reputation has become digital and everyone can see it far beyond our "village". This is how the "rating" came into being, on Fiver, on Upwork, or the number of followers on TikTok or YouTube, and so on. I believe that reliability will become an even more important value in the future. Perhaps in a few years' time, people will be able to see our rating on their augmented glasses and decide whether they can trust us with a job or the care of their children. Don't wait for such a world (a bit scary from my point of view) to take advantage of the self-amplification effects to build yourself a great reputation! Take advantage of this self-amplification effect right now to surround yourself with super-reliable people who will make your life easier. Because thanks to self-amplification effects, the more reliable you are, the more reliable people you are surrounded by, the more reliable world you live in. And conversely, the less reliable you are... If you're always late, for example, punctual people will gradually stop interacting with you. They'll prefer, consciously or more likely unconsciously, to surround themselves with people who like them, are punctual and don't keep them waiting unnecessarily. Similarly, if you keep your commitments you'll be surrounded more and more by people who keep theirs. And conversely, if you don't keep your commitments, you'll find yourself surrounded more and more by people who don't keep theirs.

The more reliable you are, the more reliable people you'll be surrounded by. In the real world and in the digital world.

My tips for getting started

We've come to the end of this part of the book where we've seen all the exponential routines, individual and collective, that you can include in your ritual of success. With your vison, your strange attractor, you now have all the tools you need to take advantage of our more chaotic world, make your dreams come true, be more resilient and even take advantage of crises... and not end up with an axe deep in the forest!

If you're having trouble deciding where to start, here's my advice.

PREPARATION

To prepare your ritual of success (allow a few hours):

- express and clarify your dream, your strange attractor, as we saw in the first chapter of this book
- write a constructive imagination verse
- write down three personal principles
- write down your express ritual

RITUAL OF SUCCESS

Start your ritual of success today! Remember, the best time to plant a tree was fifteen years ago, and the second-best time is today. The best time to start your new life is also today! To get started, you can try out a ritual of success with the following exponential routines:

- meditate or try to silence your mind for a minute
- visualize your vision, your dream for the year (or the period you've chosen)
- do your gratitude routine
- do your forgiveness routine
- visualize a constructive imagination verse
- visualize three personal principles

The whole thing should take you less than five minutes! And as usual, I'm not asking you to believe me, I'm inviting you to try (three weeks), adapt (to your context) and adopt or not (if it doesn't work, change the routines you're using).

Conclusion

You may remember the journalist I told you about in the introduction, who asked me at the end of an interview, "If there was only one thing you could do to save the world, what would it be?" So, now you know why I replied: "Say hello to your neighbor every day. Change one little thing in your relationship with others." Because what is a civilization? It's a way of living together. A set of shared rules and a vision of who we collectively are, what we've called a "strange attractor". So yes, we'll change the world with collective dreams, new narratives as we say today, and above all perhaps simply by being kinder to our neighbors, colleagues or loved ones.

I hope I've convinced you that we're living in a very special time in human history, a transition exceptional in its scale and speed. Indeed, never before in human history have so many human beings seen their lives transformed in such a short time. Our world has become more uncertain because it is more chaotic, in the scientific sense of the word. And now you know that chaos isn't a mess! There are hidden orders, the gifts of chaos:

- **the strange attractor**: even if we can't predict everything precisely, not everything happens, and you can create your own attractor, your vision, your dream
- **the butterfly effect** or self-amplification phenomenon: by changing one small thing, by setting up a small exponential routine, we can obtain immense changes, create emergences
- **Fractal images**: with the right glasses, you can recognize order emerging from disorder, for example, new fractal and less pyramidal organizations or new energy supply systems

Chaos theories show us that once the *tipping point* has been passed - and we have seen that we have passed it in many areas - our civilization can either collapse or give rise to a new equilibrium. In other words, a new civilization. And paradoxically, we've never had so much power, thanks to the butterfly effect, in this more uncertain and chaotic world.

So, either you're a billionaire and buy yourself a huge property with a bunker in New Zealand, supposedly the safest place in the world. Or, if you're less wealthy, you take several survival courses, buy bags of rice, candles and, above all, an axe to take refuge deep in the forest.

Or maybe you know that the answer to fear is not hope or optimism but courage, and you gladly choose to take part in the incredible human adventure we're being offered. Because, by now, you firmly believe in the possibility of a new more harmonious civilization emerging, if we clarify our dreams and start to put in place a new way of living together. You also know that this period, because it's chaotic, is ideal for realizing your own dreams, which you identified and clarified in Part 2, and thanks to your ritual of success you created in Part 3 of this book.

If yesterday the strong ate the weak, and today the agile swallow the rigid, then tomorrow the conscious will lead the unconscious. Together, let's create the tribe of emergeologists. And, no, we won't all end up deep in the forest with an axe!

Appendix
Why and how to prepare for crises?

"What doesn't kill me makes me stronger."
Friedrich Nietzsche

We saw in the introduction to the book that crises are the hallmark of a chaotic world. We know that, after the *tipping point*, in what we called the "self-amplifying period", more than a single crisis, we're going to experience crises in several areas (economic, social, climatic, ecological, etc.), often concomitantly and systemically. We have seen how a crisis in one area can trigger and reinforce crises in other areas. One crisis follows another. They get worse and worse. They even lead to each other. Thus, financial crises lead to economic crises, which in turn lead to social crises... which in turn lead to new economic crises, which in turn lead to political crises, and so on. These are known as systemic crises. So, how do we prepare for these crises, how do we get through them, and how do we emerge from them constructively, for ourselves, for our community and for humanity? What can we do to make the best of the economic, social and ecological crises we are going through and will continue to go through?

- You can prepare and work on both the danger and the opportunity. Indeed, a risk must be :
  - measured: what's the scale?
  - as limited as possible

- It can be "remunerated" or it can generate opportunities, improvements and progress

And while it's clear that we're going to face major social, ecological, energy, food and health crises, it's also important to anticipate major social and relational upheavals. Questions of meaning and spirituality will be more essential than ever. I propose to show you how you can better prepare for crises on these three levels: material, emotional and sensory.

Equipment and survival

How are you and your loved ones protected and able to cope with food, ecological, energy and social crises? How can you ensure your survival, that of your loved ones and that of your community? We need to ask ourselves how we can be self-sufficient in the event of a shortage in one area (energy, health, food, etc.), and how we can maneuver (mobility, communication).

The world we live in today (and probably not the "world after"...) is essentially based on two pillars: finance (or money) and oil (and fossil fuels in general). In the event of a crisis, these two pillars are bound to be the first to falter.

- Money: the slightest bank failure, even if unknown to the general public a week earlier, means a run on the cash dispensers! And no more money in them, at least for a few days, until they're refilled. So, without going so far as to put one or two million euros or dollars under your mattress, it's certainly a good idea to keep a small reserve of cash at home to cover your daily needs and those of your family.

- Gasoline: the past has shown this several times already, and the older among you will surely remember. A hauliers' strike, a few refineries on prolonged strike, and once again, the rush to the gas pumps. And once again, by a simple self-amplifying effect, the shortage quickly set in. At least long enough to fill up the tanks again! So, if you live in the countryside, far from everything, or if your activity doesn't allow you to do without your car (and if you don't yet have an electric car...), storing some gazoline, if you can do so safely, seems to me to be a good idea.

Beyond money and fuel, the usual rules of prudence are essential to be prepared for crises, be they social (such as a transport strike that would block supplies to food stores for several days), climatic (which could prevent all travel, or even prevent or damage communications), or due to health (pandemic), technological or terrorist events.

Whatever the type of crisis, it is advisable to have the basic kit at home:

- food for a few days
- an emergency medical kit
- usual medications
- a multifunction knife
- a lighter
- enough water to last a few days
- a lamp with batteries or rechargeable dynamo
- a battery-powered or dynamo-rechargeable radio
- sleeping bags
- and a good funny book to keep your spirits up
- an axe to take refuge deep in the forest (no, I'm joking!)

For more details on material preparedness for natural, health, technological and terrorist risks, check the web!

Also, to be able to seize the opportunities brought about by crises, you need to be able to mobilize resources quickly to invest in these opportunities. This can mean time or money, and especially in times of crisis you need to maintain reserves. And it's precisely when crises are approaching that you often find yourself without resources! You no longer have time to think, read or observe. So, in times of crisis, don't let yourself be overwhelmed by the hustle and bustle, and always keep some time free to seize opportunities!

Relational and emotional level

Who do you really want to keep in touch with? Which people are important to you? Do you devote enough time to them? Do you have at least decent relations with the people who surround you geographically, your neighbors, your colleagues?

> **Friends of all, enemies of all**
>
> During a visit to New York City just a few days after the events of September 11, I was struck by the radicalization of discourse and thought. In particular, it was difficult, if not impossible, at that time, and in that tragically affected place to say anything measured or questioning. It had become essential to choose a side and stick to it. Talking to friends who had lived through the war in Lebanon, they also told me how unthinkable it was not to take sides, not to choose sides at that time. If you tried to remain measured or balanced between Christians, Jews and Muslims, you found yourself the enemy of all, alone and abandoned by yesterday's friends.
>
> On a more positive note, again in New York during this period, it was amazing to see neighbors talking to each other and helping each other out after years or decades of mutual ignorance. And according to my New York City friends, the relationships forged during this dramatic period have endured for years afterwards.

In times of crisis, a neighbor's smile can warm the heart. Yours... and his/hers. It's well established that the most important parameter of resilience (from the first minutes after the tragedy) is the closeness and benevolence of loved ones (or strangers) who help overcome fears, practice healing and bring touches of joy and optimism. What best predicts a population's resilience is not damage intensity, population density or economic capital, but social capital. Before disasters strike, the key is to maintain or recreate active and frequent social ties. Within communities (neighborhoods, families, neighborhoods, ecovillages, etc.), the challenge is to learn to cultivate relationships of reciprocity and trust, as well as norms of mutual assistance. Once these norms have been established, behaviors of sharing, mutual aid, solidarity and altruism can emerge more easily during and after a shock.

So, preparing for crises on an emotional level means starting by asking yourself the following questions:

- do I know my neighbors?
- do I have their phone number? their e-mail address?
- did I invite them to dinner at least once (before the crisis)?

Crisis is also the time when you most need your nearest and dearest, your "real friends". Here too, you need to ask yourself some questions before the crisis hits:

- Who are the friends I think I can really count on?
- Am I giving them enough time and energy today?
- Have I ever made it clear that they can count on me in a crisis?

Meaning level

What's the point of going through these crises? Why are we here? How can I help the world evolve? Am I ready to contribute to the human adventure? The most mystical persons may see crises as gigantic battles between the forces of Good and Evil, or between the forces of progress and inertia! At the very least, everyone will see them as essential quests for meaning. Preparing for crises at the level of meaning means asking these existential questions before the crisis, when everything is going well. Don't wait for them to happen before starting your "self-work".

As we saw in the introduction to the book, the main ways human beings have used to understand the world are religion, philosophy and science. Depending on your own interest in each, read religious books, books on spirituality, books on philosophy, or scientific books... But above all, read books! It's probably the easiest way to prepare for crises of meaning. And if you're allergic to books, go on a spiritual retreat, take a long walk alone in nature... or, why not, watch the *Matrix* movie (again)... In short, if you want to get through and make the most of the coming crises, make sure you fill in the table below. You can even make it a fun activity with your family, friends or loved ones.

Level	Risks	Opportunities
Equipment and survival		
Emotional and relational		
Meaning and spirituality		

In summary, I invite you to take the following actions to better prepare yourself:

- have a reserve of resources, essentially time and money. You work too much, so work less! You spend too much, so build up a reserve (however small)
- identify the main risks, measure them and limit them. Prepare yourself materially by following the advice given above... and be ready to seize the opportunities!
- Set up what crisis specialist Patrick Lagadec calls the "quick-thinking force": the small group of people with whom you want to communicate and reflect in a crisis
- keep your eyes open, work on your capacity for amazement and creativity

In conclusion, I'd like to say that in the crises we're about to experience, the choice we have is between panic, saving the day and every man for himself, or solidarity, reaching out and initiating new social organizations, new relationships with ecology and nature, or with the economy. As chaos theories have shown us, every crisis can be the occasion of a collapse, but it can also be the occasion of the emergence of new ways of living, a new civilization, more in harmony with oneself, with others and with the planet. So beware of the greatest dangers as you work on your resilience:

- don't do it in fear. Do it with joy, like a game
- don't act out of selfishness. Do it with sharing in mind. One option is to stockpile rice and buy a gun to protect yourself. The other, more fun and surely more effective option is to save the money from the gun and spend it on more rice for your neighbors...
- don't do your crisis preparedness work alone. Do it with your family, your neighbors, your friends, your community. Once again, there is no such thing as resilience alone
- don't think too big. You're not preparing for a zombie attack or trying to save the world yourself. You're not Superman, you're just trying to bring some resilience to yourself, your family and your community, and that's already huge!

- don't try to find THE perfect solution. There isn't one. Just do your best. And be prepared for a lot of people to criticize what you're doing with comments like "But what if this or that happens, you're not ready for it..." Don't listen to them. In general, they haven't done anything at all to prepare themselves...

> ### The grieving process
>
> Psychiatrist and bereavement specialist Christophe Fauré revisits the stages of bereavement in the light of his long experience in psychiatric medicine and his own intense spiritual life. He describes a succession of four major temporal phases, somewhat different from the more familiar Kübler-Ross stages. I believe that knowing how to identify these different phases can help you get through crises better when you encounter them.
>
> The first is the phase of denial, shock and disbelief. Even if you've prepared for it, when death actually occurs, reason goes off the rails and refuses to admit the facts. During this phase, which takes time, anaesthetizing the emotions allows you to enter into mourning at your own pace, without letting yourself be overwhelmed, while waiting for the right conditions to be put in place for the rest of the process. It's also a time of restlessness and organization, to avoid too much confrontation with one's inner self and the pain. This is the time of collective rituals, such as funerals, which socially "validate" the entry into mourning. Then comes a powerful phase of emptiness, when we pass a point of no return by "physically" realizing the loss, through an emotional discharge: infinite sadness and the anguish of losing one's mind.
>
> The second phase, waiting, fleeing and searching, is tinged with confusion and disorientation. The inner links with the deceased are still intact, and this is expressed by flight behaviors like hyperactivity and a constant search for signs and objects linked to the deceased, in order to "find the deceased at any cost and cancel out his death, the idea of which is still intolerable".
>
> The third phase is destructuring. The pain reaches a climax when inner bonds disintegrate and landmarks disappear. The person is gripped by a great need for meaning and connection, but also sometimes by injustice, and may sink into despair, fear or anger (or nihilism or revolt against others or against themselves).
>
> The fourth phase is restructuring. This last stage is not devoid of emotion. We become aware that the scar is a sign that we have not

forgotten, and we agree to live with it. This opens up the "possibility of a return to life" and a way out of mourning. It's a time for "redefining one's relationship with others and with the world; redefining one's relationship with the deceased; redefining one's relationship with oneself". How do you find your place in a world where everything has just been devastated? Who am I, socially and intimately? In any case, there is a potential space in life where we can start something new. The final stages of mourning may lie in the search for and elaboration of this new space. It's a stage that can even be started before death, if the person has prepared for it.

Thanks

I'd like to thank all the giants whose shoulders I've leaned on to develop my own ideas and write this book. You will find them, with a few omissions, in the bibliography.

Most of the tools presented in this book were conceived and tested over many years with my friend Valentin Van Nhut, the founder of Kumiko Matcha (kumikomatcha.fr). I'd like to thank him for his friendship and complicity during these experiments and simply for being in my life.

Eliott Meunier (eliottmeunier.com) was the first proofreader of this book. His advice and friendship were with me throughout the writing process and are still with me today.

I would like to thank all the people who have placed their trust in me as a mentor, and who over the years have agreed to use my tools. They have given me the joy of witnessing positive changes in their lives and the realization of their dreams. They have allowed me to experiment and refine the tools shared in this book. Special thanks to Eliott, Ellen, Fernanda, Florent, Julien, Mathias, Samira, Yassin.

I'd also like to thank all the companies who have trusted me to let me share my ideas and tools with their employees during my keynotes.

I'd like to thank all the artists who created the soundscape that accompanied the writing of the manuscript, and more generally my life (you can find my playlist and the other book bonuses here: brunomarion.com/bonus).

And finally, I'd like to thank my parents, Gérard and Jeanne, my sister Élise and Damien, without whom I wouldn't be who I am.

Bibliography

Want to go further? Would you like to become an expert in chaos theory? Or do you simply want to continue your journey to discover the world as it is, not as it isn't anymore?

I read about 100 books a year, and I'm often asked which ones I'd recommend reading. Somehow, all these books have influenced the way I look at things... and wrote this book. So here's a list of my favorite books on these subjects.

And if you've read a book that's had a big influence on you, drop me a line - I'm always waiting for your recommendations!

Enjoy your reading!

Complexity, Uncertainty, and Chaos Theory

- Bak, Per. *How Nature Works: The Science of Self-Organized Criticality*. Copernicus, 1996.
- Elrod, Hal. *The Miracle Morning*. Hal Elrod International, 2012.
- Gleick, James. *Chaos: Making a New Science*. Penguin Books, 1987.
    - *Chaos: Making a New Science* is the book you should start with if you want to know more about chaos theory. If you want to read only one book on this subject, this is the one I recommend. The author is a journalist who has made this subject accessible to everyone.
- Hoverstadt, Patrick. *The Fractal Organization: Creating Sustainable Organizations with the Viable System Model*. Wiley, 2008.

- Gribbin, John. *Deep Simplicity: Chaos, Complexity and the Emergence of Life*. Allen Lane, 2004.
- Lazlo, Ervin. *Science and the Akashic Field: An Integral Theory of Everything*. Inner Traditions, 2004.
    - In my opinion, Ervin is one of the leading spiritual leaders (and also an artist... and a scientist...) of our time.
- Mandelbrot, Benoît. *The (Mis)Behavior of Markets: A Fractal View of Risk, Ruin, and Reward*. Basic Books, 2004.
- Mandelbrot, Benoît. *Fractals and Scaling in Finance: Discontinuity, Concentration, Risk*. Springer, 1997.
    - Benoit Mandelbrot actually invented the word "fractal."
- Merry, Uri. *Coping with Uncertainty: Insights from the New Sciences of Chaos, Self-Organization, and Complexity*. Praeger, 1995.
- Morin, Edgar. *Method (Vol. 1-6)*. Seuil, 1977-2004.
- Morin, Edgar. *Homeland Earth: A Manifesto for the New Millennium*. Hampton Press, 1999.
- Morin, Edgar. *Politics of Civilization*. Arléa, 2002.
- Morin, Edgar. *Introduction to Complex Thought*. Seuil, 1990.
- Morin, Edgar. *The Path: A New Way to Think About Everything*. Polity, 2011.
    - Edgar Morin has changed my way of seeing the world. He introduced me to the world of complexity, which then led me to chaos theory.
- Prigogine, Ilya. *Order Out of Chaos*. Bantam Books, 1984.
- Prigogine, Ilya. *The End of Certainty: Time, Chaos, and the New Laws of Nature*. Free Press, 1997.
    - He received the Nobel Prize and remains one of the few thinkers of Einstein's intellectual level. I recall with emotion reading *The End of Certainty* as if it were yesterday, and I still feel the enthusiasm of discovering a new world.
- Pryor, Robert, and Bright, Jim. *The Chaos Theory of Careers: A New Perspective on Working in the Twenty-First Century*. Routledge, 2011.

- Roddier, François. *Thermodynamics of Evolution*. Editions Parole, 2021.
- Roucoux, Katherine, and Malin, David. *Beyond the Visible: From the Atom to the Universe*. Phaidon, 2002.
  - An illustration of the fractal aspect of the world with wonderful photos.
- Taleb, Nassim. *Fooled by Randomness: The Hidden Role of Chance in Life and in the Markets*. Random House, 2001.
- Taleb, Nassim. *The Black Swan: The Impact of the Highly Improbable*. Random House, 2007.
- Taleb, Nassim. *Antifragile: Things That Gain from Disorder*. Random House, 2012.
- Taleb, Nassim. *Skin in the Game: Hidden Asymmetries in Daily Life*. Random House, 2018.
  - Sometimes I am a bit bothered by his oversized ego, but for me Nassim Taleb deserves immense credit just for the ideas in *The Black Swan* and *Antifragile*.
- Ruelle, David. *Chance and Chaos*. Princeton University Press, 1991.
  - One of the "founders" of chaos theory.
- Waldrop, Mitchell. *Complexity: The Emerging Science at the Edge of Order and Chaos*. Simon & Schuster, 1992.
- Ware, Bronnie. *The Top Five Regrets of the Dying: A Life Transformed by the Dearly Departing*. Hay House, 2012.
- Warnecke, Hans J. *The Fractal Company: A Revolution in Corporate Culture*. Springer, 1993.
- Weinberger, David. *Everyday Chaos: Technology, Complexity, and How We're Thriving in a New World of Possibility*. Harvard Business Review Press, 2019.

Sociology and Understanding the Modern World

- Anderson, Chris. *Free: The Future of a Radical Price*. Hyperion, 2009.
- Anderson, Chris. *The Long Tail: Why the Future of Business is Selling Less of More*. Hyperion, 2006.

- Asimov, Isaac. *The Last Question* in *Robot Dreams*. Ace Books, 1986.
- Bregman, Rutger. *Utopia for Realists: How We Can Build the Ideal World*. Bloomsbury Publishing, 2016.
- Bregman, Rutger. *Humankind: A Hopeful History*. Bloomsbury Publishing, 2020.
- Carr, Nicholas. *The Shallows: What the Internet Is Doing to Our Brains*. W. W. Norton & Company, 2010.
  - A good read on how the Internet is changing the way we think and process information... and how the Internet is changing the very functioning of our brain.
- Clear, James. *Atomic Habits: An Easy & Proven Way to Build Good Habits & Break Bad Ones*. Avery, 2018.
- Covey, Stephen. *The 7 Habits of Highly Effective People: Powerful Lessons in Personal Change*. Free Press, 1989.
- Diamond, Jared. *Guns, Germs, and Steel: The Fates of Human Societies*. W. W. Norton & Company, 1997.
- Diamond, Jared. *Collapse: How Societies Choose to Fail or Succeed*. Penguin Books, 2005.
- Diamond, Jared. *The Third Chimpanzee: The Evolution and Future of the Human Animal*. Harper Perennial, 1992.
  - Pulitzer Prize! I wish I had learned all this in school in History. It's never too late...
- Duhigg, Charles. *The Power of Habit: Why We Do What We Do in Life and Business*. Random House, 2012.
- Gladwell, Malcolm. *Blink: The Power of Thinking Without Thinking*. Little, Brown and Company, 2005.
- Gladwell, Malcolm. *Outliers: The Story of Success*. Little, Brown and Company, 2008.
- Gladwell, Malcolm. *What the Dog Saw: And Other Adventures*. Little, Brown and Company, 2009.
- Gladwell, Malcolm. *The Tipping Point: How Little Things Can Make a Big Difference*. Little, Brown and Company, 2000.
  - Always funny and inspiring.
- Graeber, David, and Wengrow, David. *The Dawn of Everything: A New History of Humanity*. Farrar, Straus and Giroux, 2021.

- Harari, Yuval Noah. *Sapiens: A Brief History of Humankind.* Harper, 2015.
- Harari, Yuval Noah. *Homo Deus: A Brief History of Tomorrow.* Harper, 2017.
- Harari, Yuval Noah. *21 Lessons for the 21st Century.* Spiegel & Grau, 2018.
- Heath, Chip, and Heath, Dan. *Switch: How to Change Things When Change Is Hard.* Crown Business, 2010.
- Heath, Chip, and Heath, Dan. *Made to Stick: Why Some Ideas Survive and Others Die.* Random House, 2007.
- Heath, Chip, and Heath, Dan. *Decisive: How to Make Better Choices in Life and Work.* Crown Business, 2013.
- Herrigel, Eugen. *Zen in the Art of Archery.* Pantheon Books, 1953.
- Huntington, Samuel. *The Clash of Civilizations and the Remaking of World Order.* Simon & Schuster, 1996.
- Khan, Salman. *The One World Schoolhouse: Education Reimagined.* Twelve, 2012.
  - If you don't want to read the book, at least watch his TED Talk (www.ted.com/talks/salman_khan_let_s_use_video_to_reinvent_education). A revolution in the field of education that already touches millions of people around the world. Essential if you have children... or if you don't fit into the current educational system.
- Lee, Kai-Fu. *AI Superpowers: China, Silicon Valley, and the New World Order.* Houghton Mifflin Harcourt, 2018.
- Lee, Kai-Fu, and Chen, Qiufan. *AI 2041: Ten Visions for Our Future.* Currency, 2021.
- Klein, Naomi. *No Logo: Taking Aim at the Brand Bullies.* Knopf, 2000.
- Klein, Naomi. *The Shock Doctrine: The Rise of Disaster Capitalism.* Knopf, 2007.
- Klein, Naomi. *This Changes Everything: Capitalism vs. The Climate.* Simon & Schuster, 2014.
  - It takes Naomi Klein several years to write each of her books for an absolutely incredible result. They have all changed my way of reading the news.

- Lagadec, Patrick. *Le temps de l'invention*. Préventique, 2019.
- Langlois, Matthieu. *Médecin du RAID*. Albin Michel, 2016.
- Maalouf, Amin. *In the Name of Identity: Violence and the Need to Belong*. Arcade Publishing, 2001.
    - This book greatly influenced what I wrote about fractal identity.
- Maltz, Maxwell. *Psycho-Cybernetics: Updated and Expanded*. TarcherPerigee, 2016.
- Mandela, Nelson. *Long Walk to Freedom: The Autobiography of Nelson Mandela*. Little, Brown and Company, 1994.
- Manson, Mark. *The Subtle Art of Not Giving a Fck: A Counterintuitive Approach to Living a Good Life**. Harper, 2016.
- Manson, Mark. *Everything is Fcked: A Book About Hope**. Harper, 2019.
- Margonelli, Lisa. *Underbug: An Obsessive Tale of Termites and Technology*. Scientific American, 2018.
- Marion, Bruno. *Chaos mode d'emploi*. Yves Michel, 2014.
- Marion, Bruno. *Réussir avec les Asiatiques*. Eyrolles, 2008.
- Marion, Bruno. *"S'orienter dans un monde chaotique" in Carine Dartiguepeyrou (dir.) Prospective d'un monde en mutation*. L'Harmattan, 2009.
- Meunier, Eliott. *Arrêtez d'oublier ce que vous lisez !*. Eyrolles, 2022.
- Naam, Ramez. *Nexus*. Angry Robot, 2012.
- Naam, Ramez. *Crux*. Angry Robot, 2013.
- Naam, Ramez. *Apex*. Angry Robot, 2015.
    - Among my favorite science fiction books. Visionary!
- Nowak, Martin. *SuperCooperators: Altruism, Evolution, and Why We Need Each Other to Succeed*. Free Press, 2011.
    - For all your friends who tell you that life is a race where only the strongest survive, this is the best way to learn and show them that Darwin is just part of the story. And not the most important one!
- Peters, John, and Nichol, John. *Tornado Down*. Penguin Books, 1992.

- Ramonet, Ignacio. *The Tyranny of Communication*. Le Monde diplomatique, 1999.
- Ray, Paul, and Anderson, Sherry Ruth. *The Cultural Creatives: How 50 Million People Are Changing the World*. Harmony, 2000.
  - If you have never heard of cultural creatives, you must read this book, especially since there is a good chance that you are one yourself. Therefore, it is time to discover who they are... and realize that you are not alone!
- Rifkin, Jeremy. *The End of Work: The Decline of the Global Labor Force and the Dawn of the Post-Market Era*. Putnam Publishing Group, 1995.
- Rifkin, Jeremy. *The Age of Access: The New Culture of Hypercapitalism, Where All of Life is a Paid-For Experience*. Tarcher/Putnam, 2000.
- Rifkin, Jeremy. *The European Dream: How Europe's Vision of the Future Is Quietly Eclipsing the American Dream*. Tarcher, 2004.
- Rifkin, Jeremy. *The Empathic Civilization: The Race to Global Consciousness in a World in Crisis*. Tarcher, 2009.
- Rifkin, Jeremy. *The Third Industrial Revolution: How Lateral Power Is Transforming Energy, the Economy, and the World*. Palgrave Macmillan, 2011.
- Rifkin, Jeremy. *The Green New Deal: Why the Fossil Fuel Civilization Will Collapse by 2028, and the Bold Economic Plan to Save Life on Earth*. St. Martin's Press, 2019.
- Rifkin, Jeremy. *The Age of Resilience: Reimagining Existence on a Rewilding Earth*. St. Martin's Press, 2022.
  - Jeremy Rifkin always finds a way to demonstrate major societal evolutions clearly and simply.
- De Rosnay, Joël. *Surfer la vie: Vers la société fluide*. Les Liens Qui Libèrent, 2012.
- Ruiz, Miguel Angel. *The Four Agreements: A Practical Guide to Personal Freedom*. Amber-Allen Publishing, 1997.
- Servan-Schreiber, Florence. *3 kifs par jour*. Marabout, 2019.
- Servigne, Pablo, and Stevens, Raphaël. *How Everything Can Collapse: A Manual for Our Times*. Polity, 2020.
- Servigne, Pablo, and Chapelle, Gauthier. *Mutual Aid: A Factor of Evolution*. Polity, 2020.

- Servigne, Pablo, Chapelle, Gauthier, and Stevens, Raphaël. *Another End of the World is Possible: Living the Collapse (and Not Merely Surviving It)*. Polity, 2020.
- Toffler, Alvin. *The Third Wave*. Bantam Books, 1980.
- Toffler, Alvin. *Future Shock*. Bantam Books, 1970.
- Toffler, Alvin. *Powershift: Knowledge, Wealth, and Violence at the Edge of the 21st Century*. Bantam Books, 1990.
  - I do not share his latest opinions on the world... but I still consider him one of the "godfathers" of all futurists or foresight experts, including myself.
- Willink, Jocko. *Extreme Ownership: How U.S. Navy SEALs Lead and Win*. St. Martin's Press, 2015.

Integral Theory

- Laloux, Frédéric. *Reinventing Organizations: A Guide to Creating Organizations Inspired by the Next Stage of Human Consciousness*. Nelson Parker, 2014.
  - The application of integral theory in organizations... and the best management book since Peter Drucker.
- McIntosh, Steve. *Integral Consciousness and the Future of Evolution*. Paragon House, 2007.
  - Here is one of the books to start reading (along with those by Ken Wilber) to discover integral philosophy.
- Wilber, Ken. *A Brief History of Everything*. Shambhala, 1996.
- Wilber, Ken. *One Taste: Daily Reflections on Integral Spirituality*. Shambhala, 1999.
- Wilber, Ken. *A Theory of Everything: An Integral Vision for Business, Politics, Science and Spirituality*. Shambhala, 2000.
- Wilber, Ken. *Sex, Ecology, Spirituality: The Spirit of Evolution*. Shambhala, 1995.
- Wilber, Ken. *The Integral Vision: A Very Short Introduction to the Revolutionary Integral Approach to Life, God, the Universe, and Everything*. Shambhala, 2007.
- Wilber, Ken. *Integral Life Practice: A 21st-Century Blueprint for Physical Health, Emotional Balance, Mental Clarity, and Spiritual Awakening*. Integral Books, 2008.

- Wilber, Ken. *Grace and Grit: Spirituality and Healing in the Life and Death of Treya Killam Wilber.* Shambhala, 1991.
- Wilber, Ken. *The Religion of Tomorrow: A Vision for the Future of the Great Traditions - More Inclusive, More Comprehensive, More Complete.* Shambhala, 2017.
    - Yes, I have read them all! In fact, I have read them several times. I suggest you start with *The Integral Vision*, and if you enjoy them, then you must read his masterpiece: *Sex, Ecology, and Spirituality*, one of my ten favorite books.
- Morin, Edgar, and Viveret, Patrick. *Comment vivre en temps de crise.* Bayard, 2010.
- Saloff-Coste, Michel. *Le Management du troisième millénaire.* Guy Trédaniel, 2005.
- Saloff-Coste, Michel. *Trouver son génie.* Guy Trédaniel, 2005.

Printed by Amazon Italia Logistica S.r.l.
Torrazza Piemonte (TO), Italy